Pilgrim Prayers for Leading Worship

PILGRIM PRAYERS FOR
Leading Worship

John E. Biegert

The Pilgrim Press
Cleveland

To my wife Evelyn, daughter Diane, son Douglas and his family,

and the members of First Congregational Church

(United Church of Christ) of LaGrange, Illinois,

who shared in the shaping and praying of many of these prayers.

The Pilgrim Press, 700 Prospect Avenue East, Cleveland, Ohio 44115-1100
pilgrimpress.com

Portions originally published under the title, *Listening to the Spirit: Prayers for All Occasions* (Cleveland: Pilgrim Press, 1996).

Printed in the United States of America on acid-free paper
07 06 05 04 03   5 4 3 2 1

Library of Congress Cataloging-in-Publication Data

Biegert, John E.
    Pilgrim prayers for leading worship / John E. Biegert.
        p.   cm.
    ISBN 0-8298-1567-8 (pbk.)
    1. Pastoral prayers.   2. Church year—Prayer books and devotions—
English.   I. Title.

BV250.B54   2003
264'.13—dc22

2003060871

Contents

Part 3—Invocations for Any Sunday/41

Part 4—Pastoral Prayers for the Church Year/47

Introduction

PRAYER, TO ME, is sharing our deepest feelings with God. Prayer is opening our lives to the Creator, such as when one opens the lens of a camera in order to take a time exposure. Prayer is seeking to be sensitive to God's still, small voice as we attempt to ascertain God's will for our lives. Prayer is expressing in words our hopes, our desires, our needs, our praise, our penitence.

In this book you will find a variety of prayers for a variety of uses. There are invocations and pastoral prayers that are suitable for use in services of worship throughout the Church Year, on special occasions, and on any Sunday. There are prayers that can be offered prior to church and community gatherings. Others are appropriate for expressing gratitude, seeking forgiveness, asking for guidance and help, and for use in times of tragedy and disaster.

These are prayers that I have offered to the Holy One during my ministry, and I invite you to offer them to God as printed or to use them as guidelines for your own conversations with the Divine.

ONE

Invocations for the
Church Year

Advent

Eternal God, who has given us the church and its holy days
for our preparation and inspiration; may these days of Advent
help keep us focused on whose birthday we celebrate at
Christmas time, the fact that our presence is more important
than our presents, and that we can help bring peace and
goodwill to all. AMEN.

—

O God, for whose deliverance people had been praying for
centuries, we pause in this Advent season to thank you for the
enlightenment and answer to their prayers that came to our
spiritual forebears in and through the life of Jesus. For he
indeed revealed in his life and teachings your love and amazing
grace, your will and ways, and showed humankind how to love
you by loving others as well as ourselves. May the spirit of this
Wonderful Counselor be evident in our lives during these days
before Christmas. AMEN.

—

Creator God, who comes to us again and again through the
marvels of nature, in the person of Jesus, through the voice of
conscience, and through your Spirit that dwells within us:
make us receptive during these days of Advent to your still,
small voice that calls us from childishness to childlikeness,
from fear to faith, from greed to generosity, and from a life that
is self-centered to one that is centered in you, the Ground of
our Being. For we want our lives to reflect the spirit of the one
whose birth soon will be celebrated! AMEN.

Loving and faithful God, who loves us even when we are unloving and unlovable and who does not forsake us even when we turn our backs on you; we gather to worship and praise you for this Advent season. May the meaning and message of Christmas on which we focus in these days of preparation inspire us to be more loving and faithful both to you and others. Thank you, O God, for the birth and life of the one in whom we see your love and faithfulness incarnated, even Jesus, the Christ. Amen.

—

Ever-coming yet ever-present God, we gather to prepare ourselves for the celebration of Jesus' birth. For we need your help in preventing the pace, parties, and presents of this season from crowding out the true purpose of Christmas—the rebirth in our lives of the Christ's spirit which is hope, peace, love, and joy. Amen.

Christmas Eve

God of the Babe of Bethlehem and God of each of us, like the angels of old we come into your presence proclaiming, "Glory to God in the highest!" Like the ancient shepherds we come seeking him who was born in a manger. Like the hymn writer we sing, "O holy child of Bethlehem, descend to us we pray; Cast out our sin and enter in; be born in us today." Hear our prayer, Holy One, as we worship on this Christmas Eve! AMEN.

—

With anticipation and joy we come like modern shepherds to worship on this Holy Night! We seek to be in the presence of the Christ child, for in him we see the human expression of your love and the blueprint of how you want us to live not only in worship but also in service. AMEN.

Christmas

Gracious and loving God, thank you for the gift of Christmas—the gift of your child Jesus who so enlightens us that we find in him the way, the truth, and the example of the life you would have us live. As we celebrate the anniversary of Jesus' birth into the world, may we invite your child to be born anew within us so that our lives will reflect the spirit of the Christ and brighten the lives of all whose paths cross ours. AMEN.

—

Creator God, in this Christmas season we pause to reaffirm that you have called us to give birth to the Babe of Bethlehem in our lives. We are to be the hands, the feet, the eyes, the ears, the mouth, the heart of Jesus in the world today. May this season inspire us to live in such a way that others will see the Christ in and through us. AMEN.

—

As we gather to worship today, we thank you, O God, that Christmas need not be a once-a-year celebration. Grant that the loving, giving, sharing, and caring that were evident in our lives last week will continue to emanate from us throughout the New Year! AMEN.

Epiphany

As the Star led the Magi from the East to the place where Jesus
was born; so the light of your presence, Eternal Spirit, has led
us to this place where we have come to worship you. We offer
you this day the gift of our lives as we sing our hymns of praise,
contemplate timeless passages from the scriptures, hear their
application to the living of our days, and as we pray to you in
the spirit of him who is the Light of the World, even Jesus, the
Christ. AMEN.

—

We gather, God of all Creation, on this day when we
remember that your love was revealed to and for the entire
world centuries ago on that Holy Night in Bethlehem. You
came anew not only to the shepherds in the fields but also to
the Wise Men from another country—manifesting the truth
that you are the God of us all. May our worship this day once
again etch into our minds and hearts that whether we call you
God, Adonai, Allah, or by some other name, you are the
Supreme Being of all humankind, and all are our brothers and
sisters. AMEN.

Transfiguration

Like Peter, James, and John, may we, Ever-revealing God, have a mountaintop experience today. Just as they saw Jesus in a new light, may we also gain a new perspective on his life and teachings. Just as the disciples were reminded that Jesus stood in the line of Elijah and Moses, may we realize the importance of the heroes of our faith who have preceded us. May we learn from the prophets of old, but especially from the one whom we call the Christ. For he most clearly and completely cast new light on your nature and on whom you would have us become. Amen.

Lent

We gather, O God, as pilgrims beginning our Lenten journey. During this season may we seek to learn more truths about you, more clearly discern your will for our lives, and then more faithfully live in the loving and serving manner as did the Christ in whose spirit we pray. Amen.

—

Gracious God, in whose image we have been created—the image we see personified in Jesus, the Christ—in this season of Lent we come to rededicate ourselves to follow Jesus and to be willing to deny ourselves for the sake of others. Strengthen us to help bear

the burdens of those less fortunate than we, for we know that
when we love and serve them we love and serve you. We pray in
the spirit and seek to follow the example of the one who came
not to be ministered unto but to minister, even Jesus, the Christ.
AMEN.

Palm Sunday

Eternal God, today we join the crowds of every generation
who, since the time of Jesus, have praised your name for his
coming! For his entering Jerusalem in the spirit of peace, love,
and servanthood, not as a militant conqueror, we give you
thanks. May the example of Jesus lead us to relate to you and
others in the same manner, not just today, but everyday that
the gift of life is ours! AMEN.

—

Loving God, like the multitude surrounding Jesus on that first
Palm Sunday, we often praise you with our lips but then reject
you in our hearts. Forgive us for marching to the beat of
drummers other than you. May we resolve today to be in step
with your plan and purposes exemplified in the life of Jesus,
the Christ, in whose spirit we pray. AMEN.

—

God of grace and God of glory, we praise you for Jesus who rode into Jerusalem on a donkey's colt, victorious through love and not through power or violence. Help us to learn from his example so that in living as servants and seeking to meet others at their points of need, we will find joy and give you glory. AMEN.

Maundy Thursday

Holy One, we see you most fully revealed in the life of Jesus. As we come into your presence to remember the final week of his earthly life and the last teachings he shared with his disciples, attune us anew to the last commandment he gave to them, and thus to us. For he taught on the night that we know as Maundy Thursday that as we are loved by you, we are called to love one another. Increase our love for you and others as we seek to follow the example of the Christ, in whose spirit and for whose sake we pray. AMEN.

Good Friday

We gather this day, Mighty God, in the presence of the cross of Jesus. As we stand before and beneath that cruel instrument of death, we seek to hear and understand the words that he spoke before committing his spirit into your hands. May his words before he died be transformed into living words for us, as we seek to discern their timeless lessons and carry them forth in our lives. AMEN.

Easter

O God, may we never forget the glory of Easter. To this end, stamp indelibly in our lives the meaning and message of this day: the assurance of your everlasting presence, the ultimate triumph of goodness over evil, and our possibility of new beginnings! AMEN.

—

We praise you, O God, for the glory of Easter and for its message that day will succeed night, hope will vanquish despair, peace will prevail over conflict, love will conquer apathy and hatred, and life will outlast death! May our lives be so filled with the Easter spirit that it will shine through in what we say and do, just as it shone through in the life of Jesus, the Christ. AMEN.

—

O God, with the memories of another glorious Easter still fresh in our minds, like the disciples of Jesus we gather on this first day of the week to celebrate the experience of resurrection: the promise of hope in the midst of despair, the possibility of new life before death, the assurance of continued life after death, and the reality of your spirit that is always present within and around us. May this and every Sunday be for us a "little Easter" that reminds us that Jesus is alive and that we are to be the Body of Christ in the world today. AMEN.

Pentecost

Eternal God, on this day of Pentecost we remember and celebrate the birth of the Christian Church. For those disciples of Jesus who resolved to be the ongoing Body of Christ, for those of succeeding generations who have kept the Church alive, for the many ways in which the Church ministers to us today, we give you praise and thanks. Forgive us for taking the Church for granted. And may our birthday gift to the Church be a renewed commitment to be more faithful in our worship, our sharing, and our service. AMEN.

As the disciples experienced on that day of Pentecost long ago, may we be so infused with your spirit, Holy One, that we will be overwhelmed by your presence within and among us! May we hear anew your call to be the Body of Christ wherever we live or work or play, to the end that our daily lives will reflect the life and teachings of the one in whose spirit we pray. AMEN.

Trinity Sunday

How wondrous it is Holy One, that we can experience you in a variety of ways! You are the Creator whose handiwork we see in the world around us. We can reflect upon how you want us to live and love in the person of Jesus, whom we call the Christ. We can feel your Holy Spirit tugging on our heartstrings, calling us to become the persons we can be. For making yourself known to us as Creator, Christ, and Holy Spirit, accept our gratitude. As you are One, make us one with you! AMEN.

—

O God, you are the One whom we know as Creator, Christ, and Holy Spirit. Yet in your oneness we see diversity: the God of hope, love, and peace; the Christ who fed the hungry, sought the lost, and freed the captive; the Spirit who is always within us to chide, guide, and empower. In you may we recognize and celebrate our diversity as individuals but also our unity in you, the Ground of Every Being. AMEN.

World Communion Sunday

O God, who is One, and who desires unity among earth's people, may the emphasis of this Sunday challenge us as part of the Church universal to welcome all who come to you, our Creator, in the spirit of the Christ. Let not race, color, nationality, sexual orientation, economic status, emotional or physical aptitude divide us from one another. Impress upon us anew our commonality rather than our differences. For this day we come to share in the Supper to which all have been invited—not just us and our families and friends. AMEN.

—

Sovereign of the Universe, you have the whole world in your hands and heart. You love and care about all of your creation. You desire that we who are part of the human family concern ourselves with building bridges that bring us together rather than erecting walls that separate and divide.

Thus, we thank you for this annual occasion when churches throughout the world outwardly express the tie that binds us to you and to one another. We are grateful for the life and teachings of Jesus whose example and preaching proclaims to his disciples throughout the ages that when we love, respect, and serve our fellow human beings we are loving, respecting, and serving you.

As we partake of the bread and share the cup, symbols of the life of the Christ, may we take into our lives anew his spirit. As we do so, let us remember that in him there is no East or West, in him no South or North, but one great fellowship of love through-out the whole wide earth. May we be your loving and faithful children who help to translate these words into reality! AMEN.

Reformation Sunday

God of Luther, Calvin, and Zwingli, and our God, too, on this
Reformation Sunday we gather in the spirit of your followers
long ago who sought to rescue the Church from practices they
deemed to be not in accord with your will. As we thank you
for their heritage of making available of the Bible for all to read
and of all people having direct access to you, may our worship
today inspire us to more frequently and diligently search the
Scriptures and to spend more time with you in meditation and
prayer. In the spirit of the reformers we pray. AMEN.

All Saints' Day

Compassionate and caring God, who is with us at birth,
throughout life, and at death, we gather this day to celebrate
and to remember. We celebrate that we can affirm that neither
death nor life can separate us from your love or from one
another. In the knowledge of this truth, our hearts overflow
with the memories of those who are among your great cloud of
witnesses who are with us now only in spirit. May we be
faithful to their love and heritage that never can be taken from
us. AMEN.

TWO

Invocations for Special Days

New Year's

Holy One, whose presence we keenly feel during the Christmas season and whose child Jesus we especially are inspired to follow as we celebrate his birth; may we carry the spirit of Christmas with us into and throughout this new year. Make us wise enough to know that the feelings and actions of love, generosity, involvement, and compassion that have welled within us during the holidays are to be the hallmarks of our daily lives. To make them such is our New Year's resolution! AMEN.

—

Ever-faithful, ever-loving God, who amid all the changes in life is always our Source of comfort, strength, and hope; we gather on this first Sunday of the new year to worship and praise your name. Forgive our failures of the past, and accept our gratitude for the gift of being able to begin again. AMEN.

—

Eternal, always present God, on this first day of a new year we pause to thank you for your promise always to be with us. You have been our help in the past and are our hope for the year to come. Free us from the temptation to spend too much time regretting the past, and challenge us to face the future assured that you will give us the strength needed to face whatever comes our way. We pray in the spirit of the one whose birth we just celebrated, even Jesus, our Savior, who was called Emmanuel—"God with us." AMEN.

—

Creator of Life, who ever was, is now, and ever shall be; God of change and God of new beginnings: we pause at the threshold of this new year to acknowledge that you were with us in the past and to affirm that you will be with us in the future. May our worship this day inspire us to make the most of and to put to the best use possible the new year that contains the future we will help to create. AMEN.

—

Eternal God, as a new year begins, forgive our failures of the year now passed. Sustained by our faith that you are a loving and merciful God, may we go forward into the new year resolved better to keep your commandments, to be more appreciative of your blessings, and more closely to approximate the example for living found in the one whose birth we just celebrated, even Jesus, the Christ, in whose spirit we pray. AMEN.

A Wintry Sunday

O God, we come to worship this morning confessing that the weather just about has us down! This winter has been nearly too much for us. The snow, ice, and cold have caused us to be depressed, discouraged, discourteous, and short-tempered. We have found ourselves being crabby, unloving, and unlovable. We gather, therefore, recognizing our need for the warmth of your presence and the community and support of one another. May our lives be renewed by our worship, and may we find strength to meet the challenges of this new week. AMEN.

Mother's Day

Creator God, who loves us as a father loves his daughter and who cares for us as a mother cares for her son, we gather to praise you for giving us life, to ask your forgiveness for the times when we have not used well the gift of life we have been given, and to resolve anew to be more the person you want us to be. Thank you for loving us even when we are unloving or feel that we are unlovable. We will try to do better! AMEN.

—

O God, you are to us like an ideal mother and father. You love us "although" and not just "because"; you are always willing to listen; you always stand ready to remake us. We pray to be better children of yours—willing to learn from you, concerned to be obedient to you, motivated to love you, and desirous of emulating you. AMEN.

Memorial Day

Great and Gracious God, our help in ages past and hope for years to come; we gather on this Memorial Day weekend to affirm like Paul of old that "whether we live or whether we die, we are God's" (Romans 14:8). We pause to thank you for the lives and love of those who have died and who now live with you and also continue to live within us. For their memories that always will be ours, we praise you. AMEN.

—

God of all nations and people, who desires that everyone should live together in freedom, harmony, and peace, we pause on this special day in our country to remember all who through the years gave their lives in pursuit of this goal. As we remember their example, make us good citizens who seek to do whatever we can to make ours one nation, under you, with liberty and justice for all. We pray in the spirit of him who was the Prince of Peace, Jesus, the Christ. AMEN.

Father's Day

We gather, O God, aware that today is designated as one on which to honor our fathers or their memories and also the attributes of fatherhood that we have learned from and experienced through Jesus, who called you Father. May our worship thus inspire us anew to exhibit these qualities by leading lives that are faithful, affectionate, thankful, honest, exemplary, and reverent. AMEN.

—

God, our Creator, you are to us like a father. You love us no matter what; you are continually concerned for our welfare; you seek to influence and guide us in ways that will result in our betterment; you give us freedom to grow by making mistakes as well as by enjoying successes; you always stand ready to help and listen. Thank you, O God. May we be better, more appreciative and more loving children. AMEN.

Independence Day

God of our forebears, and our God, too; we pause on this special day to offer thanks for the nation in which we live. We are grateful for those of the past whose ideals and actions gave birth to these United States. May our worship today remind us of our roots and motivate us to do whatever we can to help bring to fruition the vision of one nation, under you, where there is liberty and justice for all. AMEN.

—

Creator God, who holds the whole world in your hands, we thank you this day for the part of your world called the United States of America. But may we never forget that we are part of a global village and that all people—red and yellow, black, brown, and white—are precious in your sight. AMEN.

—

God of our mothers and fathers, we worship this day conscious of the heritage that is ours and mindful of those who conceived and gave birth to these United States. May our gratitude for their efforts and sacrifices be shown by our striving to keep burning brightly the torch they lit—a torch designed to reveal to all a nation whose sovereign is God, the One in whom we trust. AMEN.

Labor Day

From our daily labor and routines we gather on this day set aside for our corporate worship of you, the Maker of us all. We pause to profess that you created the world and all that exists therein. As we recognize this day the importance of honest labor and toil, let us not forget that our goal is not to be building bigger and better storehouses for ourselves but to use the fruit of our labor to better the world around us as well as our own lives. May this time in your presence motivate us to labor in love and service, as did the Carpenter of Nazareth, Jesus, the Christ, in whose spirit we pray. AMEN.

Christian Education Sunday

O God, Parent of Jesus the Great Teacher and our Parent; make us receptive to learning more about the one who is the Way, the Truth, and the Life. But as we learn, make us aware that we also teach by what we say and what we do. May our worship inspire us to be more receptive learners about and more faithful teachers of the Christian faith. AMEN.

Bible Presentation

Eternal God, whose Word is a lamp to our feet and a light to our paths, we thank you this day for the Bible that reveals your nature and teaches us how to live. We thank you, too, for the children who are the future of the church and the recipients of the heritage we are passing on. May our worship cause us to examine the example we set and motivate us to change if we might be causing little ones to stumble or error. AMEN.

Music Appreciation

God of harmony, who has put a song in our hearts, we have come this day to join the procession of those who have sung your praises throughout the centuries. For those who composed texts and music enabling them to be sung, we thank you. May their efforts refresh and renew us as we worship you in spirit and in truth. AMEN.

—

Creator God, Orchestrator of the Universe; you desire to be the Conductor of our lives. Thus, we gather to worship to be reminded of the score you would have us follow and to rededicate ourselves to responding to your direction and living in harmony with one another. AMEN.

Stewardship Sunday

Gracious God, we gather for worship to be reminded of who and whose we are. You are our Creator; we are your daughters and sons. You have given us: the gift of life to enjoy but not to abuse; possessions to share but not to hoard; freedom to use with responsibility but not license; talents to use but not to allow to rust. So motivate us this day that we will more fully be the persons you want us to be. Amen.

—

Ever-giving God, who has revealed that it is more blessed to give than to receive and that when we lose our lives to your will and ways we, in truth, find ourselves; make us aware of how much you have given us. During these days when we are called to financial commitment, as we have freely received let us also freely give! Amen.

—

O God, whose child Jesus taught by the example of his life that it is better to give than to receive and to minister than to be ministered unto, inspire us to adopt a stance in life wherein we are concerned not so much with what we can get but with what we can give. For it is in giving that we receive; it is in serving that we find life that is abundant. Amen.

—

We pause, great and glorious God, to express our gratitude for all that we have been given by you and by those who have gone before us. Today we offer our special thanks for all of the churches of which we have been a part that have taught us about you, enriched our lives with countless friendships, served as channels for our outreach to others, and supported us in times of difficulty and sorrow. Inspire us, we pray, to keep this church alive and vital for your sake, for our sake, and for the sake of those who will come after us. We pray in the spirit of the one whose body we seek to be—Jesus, the Christ. AMEN.

Thanksgiving Sunday

Ever-present and ever-giving God, who has given us the gift of life and its attendant blessings, as we enter this week of Thanksgiving grant us one more gift—the gift of a grateful heart. Forgive us for taking life for granted and for complaining about what we lack instead of rejoicing over what we have. May our worship today enhance our gratitude! AMEN.

—

We come to you, O God, as thankful people! We are mindful in this Thanksgiving season of our blessings, not just our difficulties; of our successes, not just our failures; of our assets, not just our liabilities; of our strengths, not just our weaknesses; of our joys, not just our sorrows. Grant us, we pray, the attitude of gratitude—not only in these coming days, but every day that life is ours. AMEN.

—

Creating, ever-faithful, ever-giving, and ever-loving God, we gladly and gratefully gather to speak and sing your praise. On this Thanksgiving Sunday we are mindful of all that you have given us. We confess, however, that too often ours is only silent gratitude, which is of no use to you or to others. Thus we pray that we will be inspired anew intentionally and concretely to reflect and express our gratitude in what we say and in what we do, as did Jesus, the Christ, in whose spirit we pray. AMEN.

—

Ever-giving and generous God, who loves us not because of our merits but just because we are; we pause in your presence, overwhelmed by our blessings. Life itself, family, friends, food, home, church, community, the marvels and beauty of creation, and other gifts too numerous to mention fill our lives to overflowing. Keep us, we pray, from ever taking for granted what we enjoy. And may we always remember that we are the caregivers and caretakers, not the owners, of all that seems to be ours. In gratitude and humility we pray. AMEN.

New Member Reception

Gracious, glorious, and loving God, whom we have come to know, love, and serve because of the Church that keeps alive the story of our faith, we rejoice today as we welcome new members into our community of faith. As they commit themselves to this local expression of your universal Church, may we recommit ourselves to being faithful members who worship regularly, contribute generously, and share as able in the life and ministry of this congregation. AMEN.

—

As we gather, loving and gracious God, we pause to reflect on the importance of this church in our lives. For the opportunities of worship, education, service, and community it provides; for the support it offers in times of crisis and need; for the ties, both old and new, that bind our hearts in Christian love; we praise and thank you. May our lives be strengthened and enriched because we have been together in this time and place. Then may we go forth to be the Church wherever we are. We pray in the spirit of the one who is the Great Head of the Church, Jesus, the Christ. AMEN.

Church Anniversary

We gather, eternal God, mindful of all that we enjoy because of the labors of others. The place where we sing your praises today was built by those who founded our church, and many of us "inherited" the chapel and sanctuary in which we regularly worship. May this service challenge us to consider what we will leave for those who will be a part of this church in the years to come. We pray in the spirit of the one who is the Cornerstone of the Church, even Jesus, the Christ. AMEN.

Church Centennial

God of our forebears and our God as well, we thank you for the gift of this local expression of the church that for a century has told the story of Jesus and his love and has ministered in the name of Jesus to people within this church and beyond its walls. May we keep alive and pass on the heritage we have been given as we gather to worship, learn, enjoy community, and then go forth to serve you by serving others. AMEN.

Congregational Meeting

We gather, O God, to reaffirm that we are the Body of Christ in this time and place, mindful that each of us members has duties to fulfill. Make us more keenly aware of our responsibilities to stay in close contact with the Body, to recognize the importance of every member, and to do whatever we can to build up this local expression of the Universal Church, whose cornerstone is the Christ. AMEN.

A Clergy Staff Person's First Sunday

With joy and anticipation we come to worship on this special day. This is a day of new beginnings in _____ Church as _____ begins (her/his) ministry among us and (as her/his family) becomes a part of our congregation! We are grateful that (she/he) accepted the call to serve as our pastor, and we pray that we, too, might accept anew our call to be committed and faithful members of this local Body of Christ. AMEN.

A Clergy Staff Person's Last Sunday

Ever-present God, we gather today mindful of the truth that
for everything there is a season. Especially are we aware that in
life there are times to say "Hello" and times to say "Good-bye".
On this Sunday when we say farewell to _____
(and _____) as she/he/they leave(s) our midst, put
in perspective our sadness as we remember with joy the
experiences we have shared during these past _____ years.
Keep her/him/them and us in your love, and remind us that we
will remain one in you and that geographic distance cannot
separate us from the ties that have bound us together. In the
spirit of the Christ we pray. AMEN.

THREE

Invocations for
Any Sunday

Invocations for Any Sunday

Breathe on us, Breath of God, as we gather to worship you. Attune our lips to sing your praises; sensitize our hearts to hear your Word; open our minds to receive your guidance; challenge our lives to emulate him whom as Christians we profess to follow. Then when the worship ends, let our service begin! Amen.

—

God of the Past, we have come to your house to reflect upon the week that just passed. God of the Present, we have come to seek your will and better understand how you want us to live. God of the Future, we have come to seek your help as we attempt in this new week to narrow the gap between who we were and whom you would have us become. Hear our prayer, for it is offered in the spirit of him who taught that we can be born anew, even Jesus, the Christ. Amen.

—

Holy, Holy, Holy are you, God of hosts! Heaven and earth are full of your glory! This morning we join millions around the world who are offering their praise and prayers of adoration, confession, thanksgiving, and supplication to you, the Holy One. As we worship you in spirit and in truth, may our lives be strengthened and become, not holier than you, but holier than they were during the past week. Amen.

—

To you, O God, we lift up our hearts! We have gathered better to know your ways and the paths you would have us take. In your goodness and love we ask your forgiveness for our sins of commission and omission and pray that we will more faithfully fulfill the covenant into which we have entered with you through Jesus, the Christ, in whose spirit we pray. AMEN.

—

O God, our light and our salvation, we come to worship you in the spirit of faith that takes away our fear, joy that diminishes our sadness, hope that overcomes our despair, confidence that overcomes our timidity. You are our strength and our shield, our shepherd and our savior. For your perennial presence within and surrounding us, we now lift our hearts in praise and prayer. AMEN.

—

Loving God, how good it is to be in this place and at this time with one another. For here among your people we would magnify and exalt your name together! Thus, may the words of our mouths and the meditations of our hearts be acceptable to you, our Rock and our Redeemer. AMEN.

—

As a deer longs for flowing streams, so our souls long for you, O God. Our souls thirst for you, the living God. For we remember the blessings that have been ours during the past week—life, love, health, food, family, shelter—and we have come to express our gratitude. Be with us in this hour as we seek to draw closer to you and as we rededicate ourselves anew to living in accord with your will and ways. In the spirit of Jesus, who is the way, the truth, and the life, we pray. Amen.

—

Creator God, you have been our dwelling place in all generations. Before the mountains were brought forth or ever you had formed the earth and the world, from everlasting to everlasting you are God. We therefore have come to your house to sing your praise, to seek your forgiveness, to open our hearts to your still small voice, and to seek more fully to align our lives with the life of the one in whom we see you revealed most clearly and completely, even Jesus, the Christ, whose name we profess and in whose spirit we pray. Amen.

—

We come into your presence with thanksgiving, Creator God, and lift our voices in songs of praise. For you are a great God and a great Sovereign above all gods. The seas are yours, for you made them. The earth is yours, for you are behind all creation. We thus worship and kneel before you, our Maker. For you are our God and we are the people of your pasture and the sheep of your hand. Amen.

—

We make a joyful noise to you, O God, and come into your presence with singing! We know, Holy One, that you have made us and that we are yours. We enter your gates with thanksgiving and your courts with praise, giving thanks to you and blessing your name. For we know that you are good, that your steadfast love endures forever and your faithfulness to all generations. AMEN.

—

O Guiding Light, whose word is a lamp to our feet and a light to our paths, we have come to this place dedicated to your worship to be enlightened. We come to hold up our lives in comparison to him who is the Light of the World. We come to learn more fully how you want us to live. We come seeking insight as to how we can serve you better. When we have been enlightened, may we go forth to be a source of light instead of shadows and darkness to those whose paths cross ours. AMEN.

—

As a candle attracts a moth to its flame; so we have found ourselves pulled to be with your people in this time and space. We realize that we cannot flee from your presence. We know the truth of the psalmist that if we take the wings of the morning and settle at the farthest limits of the sea, even there your hand shall lead us and your right hand shall hold us fast. Search us, O God, and know our hearts. Make us aware of our shortcomings. Forgive our sin, and lead us anew in your everlasting way! AMEN.

—

We gather for worship this day, Loving God, with songs of praise on our lips and prayers of confession in our hearts. We know that you are a God of Amazing Grace who will forgive our sin and renew our lives. In gratitude may we, like Isaiah of old, hear you ask, "Whom shall I send, and who will go for us?" (Isaiah 6:8a) May this service inspire us to respond, like your prophet, "Here am I; send me!" (Isaiah 6:8b) Amen.

—

Everlasting God, Creator of the ends of the earth, whose understanding is unsearchable, we come into your presence to renew our awareness that you are within and around us. You are our God who comforts us when we are distressed, who empowers us when we feel powerless, who lifts us up when we falter or fall. Thank you for the promise of your prophet Isaiah that we who wait for you shall renew our strength, we shall mount up with wings like eagles, we shall run and not be weary, we shall walk and not faint! Amen.

FOUR

Pastoral Prayers for the Church Year

Advent

O God, Christmas will he here in _____ days. This morning help us face the question of whether or not we will be ready for Christmas. But help us consider the question not from the perspective of will our presents be purchased, our cards and packages be mailed, our baking done. Rather, will we really be prepared? Will we have rethought the deeper meaning of Christmas? Will it dawn on us anew that Christmas means that you are always with us; that in Jesus we find the human example of how we are meant to live; that the greatest gifts we can give and receive are love, joy, peace, and hope?

Only _____ more days. But thank you, God that we don't have to wait. We can begin living Christmas right now! Amen.

—

Creator God, Source of all that we have and are, Sovereign of peace, Strength of our lives, Sustainer of the universe: in the humility of the shepherds and the expectancy of the Magi we prayerfully pause in your presence.

We humbly bow before you because we recognize that life and light and love came down in a special way at Christmas. We are reminded during these December days that in the one who was born in Bethlehem, we see human life as it is meant to be lived. We find light that pierces the gloom and enables us to cope with and overcome even the most difficult circumstances that come our way. And we are reminded that no matter who or what we are, we are lovable and loved by you, our Creator, and thus we can love ourselves and others.

And, Great and Gracious God, we are expectant today because we are aware that Christmas brings out the best in ourselves and in others. We know that we enjoy life much more when we and others are more concerned to: give than to receive, forgive than to harbor grudges, love than to be indifferent, cheer than to chastise.

We pray that Christmas for us will be not just a day but a spirit that we will keep alive throughout the year because we continually invite the Babe of Bethlehem to be born anew in and then to be expressed through our lives. AMEN.

—

Great, gracious, and giving God, whose gift of Jesus we celebrate during this season as we prepare for the anniversary of his birth; as the shepherds and Magi left their fields and homes to worship the Christ child, so we have come to this sanctuary to worship you.

We praise and thank you this day, O God, for the revelation of your will and ways for our lives that was bundled in the Babe of Bethlehem. For as he grew in wisdom and stature and in favor with you and others, people ever since have witnessed the incarnation of how you want us to live. How grateful we are for the human example of one: who loved you and himself enough so that he could love even those whom he did not like, who resisted the temptations that he experienced, who shared his deepest feelings and desires with you in prayer, who enjoyed the company of others because he knew that alone he was incomplete, who forgave those who wronged him, who found meaning and purpose in life by being there for others.

Forgive us for the times and ways in which, during the past week, we failed to emulate the example of Jesus. Strengthen us and renew our resolve in the days to come to give birth to Jesus' spirit, to be the hands and feet and mouth and heart—the body of Christ—as in gratitude we offer you, O God, the gift of our lives. Amen.

Christmas Eve

Creating, loving, holy God, your Spirit, will, and ways clearly and unforgettably were revealed in the life and teachings of the one whose birth we celebrate within the hour. We pause, therefore, bathed in the light of the Christmas star, to examine whether or not our lives silhouette your image in which we have been created.

This evening we would unwrap the baby Jesus from his swaddling cloths and let him grow into the one who became the Christ and our Redeemer. Thus on this Christmas Eve, we ask some Christmas questions. Jesus saw the good and the potential in others. Do we? Jesus knew that it is when we give that we receive. Do we? Jesus helped people just because they were human beings, not because of who or what they were. Do we? Jesus knew whose he was and thus sought to show his love and devotion to you by loving you with heart, soul, mind, and strength, and his neighbor as himself. Do we?

May we truly celebrate Christmas tomorrow and then keep alive the spirit of Christmas by daily emulating the one whose name we bear and in whose spirit we pray—the Babe of Bethlehem who became the Savior of us all. AMEN.

—

How easy it is to pray tonight, O God. This season, and Christmas Eve especially, makes us feel unusually close to you and to one another. Perhaps it is because Christmas heightens in us those feelings that are so in harmony with your spirit: love, compassion, joy, gratitude, expectancy, hope.

Whatever the case, we are experiencing the warmth of your and others' love; we feel motivated by your compassion to love and give of ourselves; in spite of whatever might cause us despair, there is within us an unquenchable joy; we are overwhelmed with gratitude for all that we have; we find ourselves facing confidently the future; we are engulfed by a hope that assures us that your strength will enable us to face all of our todays and tomorrows.

Keep these many manifestations of your spirit, the Christmas Spirit, burning brightly within us each day we live. And keep us ever sensitive to how and with whom we can share the light that comes from the recognition of your presence and the desire to do your will—the light that was kindled most brightly in the one who was born the Babe of Bethlehem and who became your child, our Sovereign, our Savior, and the Light of the world—even Jesus, the Christ, in whose spirit we pray. AMEN.

Christmas

O God of Christmas and of every day, God of Jesus, and our God, too; how rare is the opportunity for us to join in worship on the anniversary of the birth into the world of your child, who ever since has embodied for us a new and heightened expression of your presence and your love.

We thank you for this day for which we have been preparing for weeks. For this is the day that especially reminds us of the importance of caring, hoping, repenting, intending, sharing, thanking, meditating, adoring, and serving.

Forgive us for the occasions when these traits have been absent in our relating to you and/or others. May we keep alive within us these manifestations of the Christmas spirit not only today but in all of our tomorrows. Amen.

Epiphany

To you, Ever-Present God, we turn in prayer on this twelfth day of Christmas that historically concludes our celebration of the anniversary of Jesus' birth. As the singing of angels and the adoration of shepherds fade into the background, we pause to remember what down through the centuries has been commemorated on Epiphany, which is observed tomorrow. Thus, as the season of Epiphany begins, we remember again your manifestation in the birth of Jesus that inspired the Wise Men from the East to follow a star to the stable where they found the Christ.

Forgive us, O God, for not being as wise as they: for those times when we flounder and go around in circles rather than having a goal in our lives; for those occasions when we think we know it all and are unwilling to ask for direction; for the low priority we often give to offering gifts to the Christ-child and thus to you—gold, our financial resources; frankincense, a symbol of worship; myrrh, used to minister to people in pain.

As we go forth from this place filled with the reminders of your abiding love, amazing grace, and the power to become whom you want us to be, revealed in the life of the Babe of Bethlehem, may we be wise enough to carry with us into this new week and new year, the assurance that we can indeed be like the Wise Men of old. AMEN.

Transfiguration

God of Life and Love, God of New Beginnings, hear the prayers of your people this day. As we commemorate that day long ago when Jesus' beloved disciples were granted a deeper understanding and new appreciation of his nature and personhood, may that same experience be ours.

The disciples learned that you have been revealing yourself throughout the ages in human beings like Elijah and Moses who sought to teach people about you and who sought to follow your leading. May we also seek to have our lives count for you.

The disciples learned that Jesus is the Christ, the one who most fully reveals your nature, your will, and your ways. May we look more often into the mirror provided by the life of Jesus, seeking to discern how closely our lives conform to his image and promising anew to align our words and deeds with his.

The disciples learned that life is not a continuous mountaintop experience and that they soon had to descend the mountain and return to their daily routines. Remind us that we soon will leave this place of worship and return to our homes, offices, and settings of work and leisure. May we carry with us the inspiration of this day. As we are now fulfilling your commandment to remember the Sabbath to keep it holy, may we not forget the weekday to keep it holy as well! Amen.

Lent

Great, gracious, and giving God; Confidant of the confessing, Healer of the hurting, Help of the helpless, Hope of the hopeless, Light of the lost, Lover of the loveless, Savior of the sorrowing; when we pause long enough to consider who you are and how you have enriched and undergirded our lives, we are humbled by the realization of how great you are and how amazing is your grace!

Yet, in spite of your goodness to us, we too often take you for granted and admit you only to the periphery of our lives. We think of you periodically; we follow you halfheartedly and haphazardly; we love you lukewarmly.

Faithful Father, Marvelous Mother, Pardoning Parent; our prayer this morning is that we will be more intentional about our Christian living. May the season of Lent that we enter this week be a time when we more consciously practice your presence—asking ourselves: What would Jesus do in this situation? How would he relate to this person or that?"

May we be more faithful followers of the one whose name we profess, ones who practice what we believe and preach, and among those who show others, not tell them, the way! AMEN.

—

Living God of all who live, for whose spirit we long, to whose voice we would listen, and from whom we would learn; we pause in your presence in this Lenten season.

Educate, empower, encourage, energize, and enlighten us as we embark on our journey designed to enable us more efficaciously to emulate the empathetic example of Jesus.

Nudge us so that we will not be so nonchalant about these noteworthy days. May we never neglect our need for nurturing so we can be more than nominal disciples.

Transform our tendency to thirst for the trite and trivial. Turn our thoughts, O Transcendent One, toward trying to temper our lives with the timeless traits of tenderness, thankfulness, thoughtfulness, and truthfulness.

Creator God, we love you; we embrace you; we need you; we trust you. AMEN.

—

Creative and Creating God, whose artistry that blanketed the earth with snow this past week is symbolic of the way in which your love blankets our lives, we come to offer our lives in worship—not because we must but because we may, not because we have earned your love but because you love us just because we are, not because we seek to be exceptions to the human race but because we seek strength for facing the difficulties that are a part of being human.

As we thank you for your love and presence within and around us, we confess that sometimes we have been unloving toward and not present for others. For being apathetic rather than active, critical rather than caring, disdainful rather than devoted, griping rather than grateful, petulant rather than peaceful, neglectful rather than nurturing, spiteful rather than supportive, thoughtless rather than thoughtful, forgive us.

As we move toward the conclusion of Lent and anticipate the celebration of Easter, may Easter's message of the hope of new life before death become a reality as we strive to live our lives as Jesus lived—as your children who, knowing that we are loved, love you, ourselves, and others. AMEN.

—

God of winter and God of springtime, who created the universe with its changing seasons, we in your church thank you for the season of Lent. For in these days we have been learning more about how you want us to live by reflecting on the life and teachings of Jesus.

Today we especially thank you for his life. For here was a human being like us who was so sensitive to your will and who so used his potential that he became the example of full humanity. Jesus learned and practiced the truths: that in your will is true peace, that your strength enables us to cope with life, that good can come from evil and tragedy, that there is hope in the midst of despair, that love is the most powerful force in the world.

As Jesus matured and grew in his relationship with you to the point where these truths became part and parcel of his daily living, may we similarly hunger and thirst for this goal. For you have created us for yourself, and we are restless and unfulfilled until we are consciously committed to you. AMEN.

Palm Sunday

With the memory of that first Palm Sunday engulfing our minds and hearts, we feel that we are part of the assemblage walking with Jesus on the winding road down the Mount of Olives into the Holy City of Jerusalem. In our minds' eye, we envision ourselves waving palm branches and shouting, "Hosanna to the Son of David! Blessed is the one who comes in the name of God! Hosanna in the highest heaven!" (Matthew 21:9b) May we be modern Palm Sunday pilgrims who strive to follow Jesus and offer allegiance to his teachings and example.

With concern, however, we remember how the majority of the Palm Sunday crowd deserted Jesus when the going became difficult. They were unwilling to stand up for him in the presence of others. The "Hosanna" cries of some even turned into cries of "Crucify him!"

We confess, O God, that at times, we have deserted the namesake of our faith. For disregarding his teachings to love you with heart, soul, mind, and strength; for not loving our neighbors as ourselves; for failing to seek first your realm and your righteousness; for concentrating on building bigger and better barns for ourselves and neglecting those in need; for glossing over the importance of the Sabbath and our corporate worship, grant us your forgiveness.

May we go forth into this Holy Week seeking to be more holy ourselves and better followers of the Christ whom we honor this day! AMEN.

Maundy Thursday

God of Jesus, the Christ, and our God, too, on this holy day (evening), we gather for worship in the spirit of remembrance. We are transported back in time to the occasion when, shortly before his death, Jesus shared a meal with his disciples in an upper room in Jerusalem. We recall how, in an act of humility, Jesus washed the feet of his disciples. In our minds' eyes, we see Jesus blessing bread and wine and then sharing them with his close friends saying, "Do this in remembrance of me" (Luke 22:19b). We hear him instructing his disciples, "This is my commandment, that you love one another as I have loved you" (John 15:12).

We follow Jesus to the Garden of Gethsemane where he shared his deepest feelings with you in prayer. We feel the sadness and pain Jesus felt when one of his disciples betrayed him and another denied him. We feel the agony that was his when he was subjected to the mockery of a trial.

Forgive us, gracious God, for the times when we have failed to love one another as you love us. Forgive us for denying or betraying you by our words or actions. Forgive us for not often enough sharing our deepest feelings with you in prayer.

May this service motivate and energize us to be more loving and faithful followers of the Christ by whose name we call ourselves and in whose spirit we pray. Amen.

Good Friday

Transforming God, by whose powerful love a dark, dastardly, deadly day became a good Friday, near the end of this Holy Week we pause to ponder the meaning and message of this day on which we commemorate Jesus' crucifixion. In the spirit of reflection and introspection, we confess that at times our lives have, in effect, cried out, "Crucify him!" For broken relationships with you and others, for failing to walk the walk that we sometimes glibly talk, for forgetting to ask ourselves what Jesus would do in certain situations, for taking lightly or ignoring our responsibilities as members of the Body of Christ, grant us your forgiveness.

Thank you, God of Life and Love, for what we can learn from that first Good Friday. We learn the depth of Jesus' love for you and his followers then and now in his willingness to fulfill the role of Messiah—a love that was faithful unto death. We learn the importance of forgiving others, even when they mistreat us. We learn to seek to discern how we are meant to live, even when it might mean our choosing a difficult or sacrificial path. We learn to commit our spirits to you, the Ground of our Being, in life but also in death.

For these lessons of Good Friday and for the fact that we know that a brighter and glorious day lies ahead with its message that there is life even beyond and in spite of difficulties and death, we are eternally grateful. Accept the rededication of our lives to you and the one in whose spirit we pray—even Jesus, the Christ. AMEN.

Easter

Ever-beckoning God, you continually call us from: apathy to action, callousness to caring, faithlessness to faithfulness, greed to generosity, haughtiness to humility, hopelessness to hope, meaninglessness to meaning, sadness to solace, sin to servanthood—in other words, from death to life. Forgive us for so often not heeding your call and remaining in the ruts that sink life below what it might and can be.

Thank you for Easter. For its message is that we can grow and change; we can rise to higher planes of personal living; there is hope in the midst of our despair; there is joy in spite of sadness. As Jesus' tomb stood open on that first Easter morning, on this Easter may our lives stand open to your spirit that can breathe into us newness of life. Fill us with the radiance of this day so that your love may stream in and through us, bringing light and life to a world that often walks in shadows and death. AMEN.

—

Eternal, ever-loving, ever-present God of Easter and our everyday existence:

Accept our accolades and ascriptions of awe and adoration as we assemble in this sanctuary today.

Save us from a saccharine, sanctimonious, social celebration of what should be a saving, spiritual, and symbolic Sunday and season.

Thank your for Easter's teaching and truth that temptations, testings, troubles, trials, and tragedy can be transformed into triumph.

Enable, energize, and empower us to the end that the evidences of Easter will be embodied and exemplified in our lives.

Reawaken, renew, and redirect us so that we might rededicate ourselves to realizing the resurrection that reposes in our lives and desires release. AMEN.

Pentecost

Ever-Revealing God, whose spirit descended centuries ago on the early disciples on the day of Pentecost like a burst of mighty wind, we gather on the anniversary of that occasion to seek anew the infusion of your spirit. We recall how your spirit enabled people, though speaking different languages, to understand one another. We recall how your ever-beckoning spirit inspired and motivated people from different cultures and countries to be baptized and become part of a new movement now known as the Church. We recall how these newly committed people, aware that Jesus no longer was physically among them, determined to be the Body of Christ seeking to carry on his ministry and mission.

Remind us this day, O God, of our heritage. Remind us that, although dissimilar in terms of race, nationality, culture, gender, sexual orientation, age, physical and mental capacities, and specific beliefs, we are one in seeking to be the Church in this twenty-first century. May we be modern baptized and committed Pentecost people—a local expression of the universal Church committed to being the hands, feet, tongues, and helpers of the Christ whose name we profess and in whose spirit we pray. AMEN.

Trinity Sunday

Triune God, our Creator, Redeemer, and Sustainer, we come to worship you whose reality we experience in different ways. As we look at the worlds around us, we are overwhelmed by your creative genius. Truly the heavens and the earth reveal your infinite glory and impress upon us our finite nature. We sing with the psalmist, "When I look at your heavens, the work of your fingers, the moon and the stars that you have established; what are human beings that you are mindful of them, mortals that you care for them?" (Psalm 8:3–4)

Yet, we are filled with the assurance that you have redeemed us from meaningless existence, for we have been created in your image. You have given us power to love, freedom to choose, intellect to reflect, the ability to change, and settings in which to serve.

When, O God, we use unwisely these gifts that are ours, when we confess and ask for forgiveness for being less than we were created to be, you are present to guide and sustain. You enable us to begin again and to keep on keeping on!

May we seek to become one with you and with one another as we enter this new week. And may we be ever mindful of who and whose we are! We pray in the spirit of the one in whom we experience your amazing, sustaining grace, even Jesus, the Christ. AMEN.

Reformation Sunday

God of Amazing Grace and Glory, we pause to commemorate the movement that nearly five hundred years ago changed Christendom for all time. Today we celebrate the lives of those reformers who, while being true to the essentials of the faith, recognized that it was time for changes to be made.

Thus, we thank you for their insight that our justification comes through our faith in you that is to be the basis for the good works we undertake. Our forebears perceived that since all of us have sinned and fallen short of your will for our lives, it is your love and grace, not our works alone, that restore us to a right relationship with you.

We thank you, too, that the Reformation unchained the Bible that at one time was the sole province of the Church. Now we can, with the minds you have given us, read and interpret the scriptures individually and with one another, seeking to discern what we understand to be your Word for our lives.

Finally, accept our gratitude for those reformers who realized that, whether ordained or laity, none is better than another and that each of us has direct access to you. For we now know that there is a priesthood of all believers—each having the liberty to offer her or his sacrifices of time, talent, and resources directly to you.

As we thank you for these gifts from the reformers of old, keep us ever alert to reforms that might be needed in our local church today. Wherever and whenever we become aware of ways in which our local expression of the Body of Christ might be a more efficient and effective agent in your realm, make us bold enough to take a stand and work toward those ends.

In the spirit of the Christ, who calls us from passive to active discipleship, we pray. AMEN.

All Saints' Day

Everlasting God, you are our help in ages past and our hope for years to come. You are our shelter from the storms of life, and our eternal home. On this poignant day our thoughts focus on those who from their labors rest, who now abide in your eternal realm, but who also are etched indelibly in the walls of our personal halls of memory.

As we stroll down this hallway found in our hearts and minds, we remember family members, friends, and others who have preceded us in death but who also continue to live within us. For the love they showered upon us, for the variety of gifts we received from them, for their examples that offer patterns for our lives to follow, hear our words of gratitude and praise.

Grant that ours will not be empty or meaningless words, but words that are woven into the very fabric and actions of our lives. May we be faithful and true to what we have been given by those whose lives we celebrate this day. And, O God, may we keep their memories green! AMEN.

FIVE

Pastoral Prayers for Special Days

New Year's

O God, whose commandments we would keep, whose community we would enjoy, and to whose service we would be loyal, we pause before you as we cross the threshold of another year. For its open doors of possibilities and its hope of new beginnings, we give you thanks.

We are especially grateful that at the core of our faith is the message that life is a matter of becoming and that we can begin again. We confess that there is some of the year just passed that we would like to forget and erase: words that hurt rather than helped, acts that we know were sinful. Some of these blots and stains we can remove by corrective action in the days to come, and we pray from you the desire and strength to right these wrongs. But some of our mistakes are irreparable, and all we can do is sincerely to ask your forgiveness while at the same time vowing not to repeat our errors of the past.

So thank you for the new page in our lives. May the entries we make on it be in harmony with your design for us. And months from now may we be more satisfied with this year's page than last year's. For it is a reasonable expectation that we should be better and worthier at the end of the year than we are at the beginning! May this be our goal. AMEN.

A Snowy Sunday

O God, to what a beautiful day we awakened! The snow blanketing the ground and hanging on trees and shrubs is a majestic sight, and what symbolism it evokes! Like snow, your love blankets our lives. Just as the snow covers the ruts, potholes, and debris that dot our streets and lawns, just as it covers the barren winter landscape, so your love offers us the opportunity to rid ourselves of the blemishes in our lives. If we seek your forgiveness and strive to begin anew:

- the ruts of bad habits can be smoothed out;
- the potholes bred by indifference and apathy can be filled;
- the debris of self-centeredness, fractured relationships, and lack of concern for others can be cleaned up.

But, O God, if we are living with no regrets, no desire to change for the better, no sense of needing your forgiveness, our pride begins to melt the blanket of love with which you desire to refresh, restore, and beautify our lives. Just as the white melting snow loses its luster and beauty, so the ruts, potholes, and debris in our lives begin to show their ugly heads again!

Ever-beckoning God, may we carry away from this house of worship in our mind's eye the picture of this beautiful day to remind us that your love is available to cover our lives, if we will let it. May the picture also remind us that we can be forgiven and our lives made new! For deep in our hearts we know the truths affirmed by the prophet Isaiah, "Though your sins are like scarlet, they shall be like snow" (1:18b), and by the Psalmist, "Wash me, and I shall be [cleaner] than snow" (51:7b). Amen.

Martin Luther King Jr.'s Birthday

God of the universe and of all people, Parent of the human family in which we are sisters and brothers of one another, we pause to offer our special prayers prior to a significant national holiday.

You have called us, O God, to be dreamers of dreams and to dream that one day ours indeed will be one nation, under you, with liberty and justice for all. We confess, however, that we dream too much and act too little. We are not always color blind. We accept and judge others on the basis of how they are different from us, thus erecting barriers because of race, class, creed, or sexual orientation. We forget that red or yellow, black, brown, or white, all are precious in your sight.

Thank you, God, for people like Martin Luther King Jr.—those who in the past and even today challenge us to ensure that none will be denied life, liberty, or the pursuit of happiness; none will be denied justice or opportunities. For all of us are persons, not pigmentations! Amen.

Super Bowl Sunday

God of grace and God of glory; Fountain of light and truth; Lover of every soul; Source of all that we are and have; Sustainer of our lives: we have gathered for worship on a super day as well as Super Sunday.

We confess, Holy One, that often we become confused about what is important in life and that our priorities are all mixed up. There are times when we feel that football is as important as faith, when games are of more interest that grace, when huddles attract our attention more than homelessness, when plays have more stature than prayer, when coaches seem on a par with the Christ, when success can be substituted for sportsmanship, when salaries make us forget about stewardship, when touchdowns are equated with theology.

Restore us to our senses, O God. Let us remember that persons are more important than points, that serving is more important than Super Bowls, that worship is more important than winning, and that the love we experience coming from you and one another enables us to get through the periodic losses that come our way in life. AMEN.

Abraham Lincoln's Birthday

Gracious and glorious God, whose principles for living have been exemplified by a great cloud of witnesses who have gone before us, this morning we are especially reminded of the historic hero whose birth is remembered this weekend. From the life of this man who became president of our nation and preserver of the Union we can learn so many lessons: the value of working diligently to achieve our goals, the need to try again when we fail, the strength that comes from hope, the immorality of discriminating against another person because of the color of his skin or her station in life.

As Abraham Lincoln was called the Great Emancipator, help us not to forget that you, O God, are the greatest emancipator. For when we earnestly seek to follow your intention for us, when we consciously attempt to model our lives after that of Jesus: we are set free from the bondage of sin; we are saved from an existence that has little or no meaning to a life that has purpose and direction; we are delivered from fear and filled with hope; we are given the grace to forget the past, begin again, and keep on becoming.

Thank you for standing ready to help us be freed to become more fully human and to actualize more completely the love, compassion, and penchant for serving you and others that wells within us but whose floodgates we need to open wider. May the realization of more of our potential be our goal today and every day that we are privileged to live. Amen.

Valentine's Day

God of Love, whose love was best illustrated long ago in the way Jesus of Nazareth loved you and those with whom he shared life, we pause in your loving presence to reaffirm that you are our God and we are your people, to be reminded that you are like an ideal loving parent, and to reassess our lives in the light of your love.

Thank you for loving and caring for and about us. Forgive us for the times when we have failed to love you and others as we know we should. We confess that too often we take you for granted and forget that there are some rules and regulations by which you would have us live; too often we think that if we do not like someone we are excused from loving that person; too often we view others as objects and not persons, thus demeaning and dehumanizing them.

O God, on this day associated with love, make us better lovers of you and one another. Help us to notice, help us to care, help us to be available to any person in need. For in loving others we love you, in serving others we serve you, in ministering to others we find our lives strengthened and enriched. AMEN.

Presidents' Day

Sovereign of the Universe and Creator of all, we pause during this holiday weekend to recognize and pay tribute to all who have served as President of the United States of America throughout its history. For their willingness to serve and their contributions to our nation, we express our gratitude.

We pray your blessings upon those who served in our nation's highest office and now continue to serve in other ways as well as for President _____ who now occupies the White House. Amid all of the difficult decisions he continually faces, may he be sensitive and receptive to your divine guidance so that his leadership will embrace the qualities that our nation long has professed. Remind him and us again and again that our trust is to be in you, that our goal is to be one nation, under you, and that continually we are to strive to make ours a nation where there is liberty and justice for all.

Where we as a nation fall short, forgive us all. In your grace, grant us the motivation to work intentionally and diligently toward the goals we espouse. We pray in the spirit of him who gave his ultimate allegiance to you—Jesus, the Christ. AMEN.

Earth Day

Creating God, Creator of the planets, the sun, the moon, the stars, and of life itself; we, the epitome of your creation, pause to worship you with words and songs of praise! You are our God; we are your people; and we have come to affirm this fact!

Yet, Eternal Spirit, we confess that we do not always live as though we are yours. You created us to care for one another and the world in which we live. Too often, however, we uncaringly treat others as things to be used, and we thoughtlessly abuse the world into which we were born. Forgive us, we pray.

Thank you, God, for Earth Day and for its reminders and challenge for each of us to be better caretakers of the planet you have entrusted to us. Inspire us this day to be better citizens of this earth: who seek to conserve and not waste exhaustible natural resources, who do not spoil the beauties of nature by littering or trashing, who urge our elected officials to curtail deforestation and pollution.

May we go forth from this place with the words of clergyman Edward Everett Hale ringing in our ears and informing our lives: "I am only one, but still I am one. I cannot do everything, but still I can do something; and because I cannot do everything I will not refuse to do the something that I can do." AMEN.

—

Gracious God of the universe, who has the whole world in your hands, we, your children, the highest form of your creation, pause in your presence to share with you our deepest feelings in this time of prayer. There is so much going on around us, and as we pause to sort out the world in which we live we realize that there is much that we need to appropriate into our lives.

Earth Day has come and gone. But, Creator God, keep us ever aware that you have entrusted to us the care of our planet Earth. You have given it to us to use but not to abuse. Our world has natural resources that we are to conserve for the world of our children and our children's children, resources that we are not to deplete just for the sake of our own pleasure or comfort. Thus, make us so responsive to conservation and recycling that every day will for us, in a sense, be Earth Day.

We live in a day and age when Hollywood and television seem to create for our nation's children, and sometimes for us, heroic figures and role models. Thus, O God of love, may those with penchants for self-centeredness, force, violence, and destructiveness not become characters whom we seek to honor or emulate. Rather, O Holy One, who continually beckons and who always responds to the invitation to enter our lives, make us as desirous to find your will for us and the insights provided for our daily living that are found in the Bible as we are concerned to find the answers to the crossword puzzles that appear in our daily newspapers.

Finally, O God, our help in ages past and our hope for years to come, hear the silent prayers we offer for persons who are especially near and dear to us and for situations in which we have a particular interest. AMEN.

Daylight Savings Time

God of the past and future, God of the changing seasons; we have gathered in this place dedicated to your worship after a night made shorter because one hour passed in an instant. That hour, O God, is gone and cannot be recovered.

We did not have an opportunity to use wisely or to waste that hour. But, O Source of life, there are so many other hours that are at our disposal. We thank you for them, and we also ask your forgiveness for those hours that we have used and continue to use unwisely.

We confess, Pardoning Parent, that we waste so many of our hourly gifts: by looking for faults in other people; by holding on to grudges; by postponing those good deeds that we think about doing, with the result that they remain only good intentions; by being so consumed with our work that we neglect our families, friends, and faith; by spinning our wheels rather than making a decision and moving on with our lives.

Enable us, we pray, to make better use of our gift of life's hours: by taking time to observe the beauty of the earth in springtime; by being alert to and responding to the needs of others, including our family members; by spending some time each day in meditation, reflection, and prayer; by giving back to you at least one hour each week in which we join others in offering you our praise and thanks; by doing at least one thing each week that will make our world a better place in which to live.

Thank you, God, for this and every hour of our lives! AMEN.

Mother's Day

O God, whose children we are and who is like a parent to us, we have come to worship you on this special day that reminds us of the importance of the families of which we have been and are now a part.

Many of us have so much for which to be grateful. For parents who gave us birth and nurtured us with love; for sisters and brothers with whom we have shared many experiences; for a husband or wife whose very life gives meaning, purpose, and fulfillment to our own; for sons and daughters whom we love and in whom we have invested ourselves; thank you!

Heavenly Parent, help us realize how much poorer we would be without these relationships. Therefore, may we not take them for granted but do all within our power to strengthen, enrich, and preserve them. Amen.

Memorial Day

God of us who are living and those who have preceded us in death, you whose we are whether we live or die, our hearts are overflowing with the gift of remembrance as we worship you this day. How great and humbling is our debt to the past and to those present with us now only in our memories. For the lives of those to whom this day we dedicate lasting memorials that will enhance the ministry of our church and for others near and dear to us who now from their labors rest, we give you thanks. For those who throughout the history of our nation have given their lives in behalf of freedom, justice, and peace, we express to you our gratitude.

Guide and sustain us, O God, as we receive their inheritance, defend it, invest it, and share it with the world. Keep us faithful to the qualities of personhood and nationhood that are acceptable to you so that we, too, may leave for others a heritage that is imperishable and undefiled. AMEN.

A Rainy Sunday

Bountiful Creator, you are the God of thunder and lightning, whose clashing and flashing speak of your presence around us. You are the God of rain whose showers—sometimes in gentle raindrops, sometimes in cascading downpours—speak of your blessings that flood our lives. We therefore pause in our worship as even now our earth is being refreshed to offer to you our prayers of praise.

As the rain calls forth seeds that turn into blades of grass and buds that are transformed into flowers, so it calls forth from our lives expressions of gratitude for the ways in which our lives have been blessed. For life itself, for families and friends, for food and shelter, for health and material resources, we offer our thanks. For your amazing grace and forgiving love that accept us in spite of and not just because, we thank you. For your continual presence that strengthens us for the living of each day, for the gift of hope, for the ability to cope, we express our appreciation.

When life becomes tough, when the going is rough, save us from despair. Let not the umbrella of forgetfulness prevent us from remembering and being refreshed by the showers of blessings that are ours. In the spirit of another of your gifts to us, Jesus, the Christ, we pray. Amen.

Confirmation

Creating and loving God, we pause in your presence on this day of Confirmation—the day when _____ of your children make promises to enter into a covenant with you and this church.

Our prayer this day is one of gratitude and petition. We offer our thanks for these young people soon to be confirmed and for their families. We thank you for the time and energy these youths have invested to prepare themselves for this hour when they consciously and publicly accept the Christian faith as their way of life and when they become official members of the Church—the body that seeks to carry on the mission and ministry of Jesus, the Christ.

We pray that they will take seriously the commitment they make this morning and that their families and we, their friends, will offer our support and encouragement to the end that they will feel this to be a day of spiritual significance and not simply the fulfillment of a social custom. May these confirmands not forget, but be faithful to, their confirmation vows.

But, O God, our prayer also is one of confession. We who are members of your Church confess that we often forget or take lightly the vows we took and the promises made when we embraced the Christian faith and became a part of a local expression of the Body of Christ. The activities of our daily living and our being faithful members of the Church often have been less than exemplary. Forgive us, and as once again we hear promises made and vows accepted, may we reaffirm them in our hearts and rededicate ourselves to being more faithful and effective witnesses of your presence and love in our world. AMEN.

Teacher Appreciation

Great Shepherd, who loves and cares for us as a shepherd cares for a flock, we pause to acknowledge and praise you for the fact that all of us—no matter who we are, whatever our race, religion, ethnicity, class, or sexual orientation; in spite of our faults and sinful ways—are a part of your flock. You have created us! We are yours! Thank you!

Forgive us for the times when we have strayed from your presence in words or deeds. And may our worship today inspire us to rededicate ourselves to follow you more faithfully and not to lose contact with your Holy Spirit. For you are the Ground of our Being, and in and from you we receive guidance and direction, strength to cope with whatever comes our way, and healing for the hurts that are a part of life.

We are especially grateful this day for those of our church who have been teaching these truths to our children and youth during this church school year. We thank you for their commitment and dedication to helping their students learn about our faith—a faith that always is only one generation away from extinction if it is not taught by and caught from us and others.

Hear this prayer that is offered in the spirit of the one who also was like a shepherd to those who followed, even Jesus, the Christ. AMEN.

Father's Day

O God, on this particular day to call you Father has special significance. For today we pay tribute to our fathers or their memories, and we are especially mindful of the attributes of fatherhood. Yes, many of us are thinking with gratitude of that man who has or had such great influence on his or her life, that man who seeks or sought to embody the ideals of fatherhood.

For what is a father? A father is: fair, faithful, and forgiving; able, accepting, and authentic; temperate, thankful, and thoughtful; honest, honorable, and hospitable; embracing, empathetic, and exemplary; reasonable, receptive, and responsive.

As we thank you for these qualities in our fathers we are grateful that they are your attributes, too. And, O God, we pray that these same traits also might be evident in our lives. Amen.

Independence Day

God of all the nations, Parent of all humankind, Good Shepherd of all who will follow you; as we approach the anniversary of the birth of our nation we are mindful of the heritage we enjoy as citizens of these United States of America. For those who created a new republic sought to base it upon the foundation of noble ideals. They affirmed that you are the Supreme Judge of the world. They affirmed that all people are created with equal and in alienable rights, including life, liberty, and the pursuit of happiness.

We confess, however, that all too often we have forgotten or forsaken the heritage entrusted to us by our founding fathers and mothers. Instead of making you our Supreme Judge we have followed the dictates of our own consciences, even when they conflicted with your divine will. Our guidelines more and more have become "Is it good for the economy?" or "Is everyone else doing it?" rather than "Is it right or wrong?" And instead of recognizing all people as your children and that we are all brothers and sisters, we have discriminated against and put down those who differ from us in color of skin, or in sexual orientation, or in religious faith, or in economic status.

Forgive us. And as we celebrate the birth of our nation may each of us resolve to do a better job of making ours one nation under you, with liberty and justice for all. AMEN.

—

Wise and wonderful God, Creator of the universe and Ultimate Source of life's blessings, we pause in awe and humility as we ponder your greatness and your goodness. We are amazed at the world in which we live, with all of its natural resources and its natural laws that have brought order out of chaos. We are humbled by the miracle of birth and life, for they remind us that there is a power greater than we.

As we approach another anniversary of the birth of our nation, we give you thanks for the heritage that is ours. For the Native Americans who saw you in the forces of nature—sun, moon, stars, clouds, rain—and who sought to conserve the land and animal life, we thank you. For the Pilgrims who uprooted themselves from their homeland and came to these shores so they could be free to worship in ways meaningful to them, we thank you. For the founders of our nation who affirmed "In God we trust," we thank you.

This morning we ask you to forgive us for not taking better care of those who were here before the colonists arrived and for too often despoiling the beauty and wasting the exhaustible resources of land and animal life. Forgive us, too, for taking for granted our freedom to worship, that too often results in our neglecting this facet of life. And forgive us for putting our trust in the many gods that sometimes crowd you off center stage— the stock market, the games we play, our penchant to please ourselves instead of you.

As the Fourth of July dawns, may it dawn upon us that from time to time we need to examine our heritage and do a better job of caring for others, caring for our God-given resources, and caring about you! Amen.

Labor Day

Creator God, the Labor Day weekend is a fascinating one! It reminds us of the work we are privileged to do and by which we earn our daily bread. It provides a holiday on which we can relax from our usual labor and play. It contains this Sunday when we can come to your house to spend an hour worshiping you.

This morning, however, we confess that our lives are not as integrated and whole as we would like them; our relationships are not as meaningful and satisfying as we desire. Help us to understand that this is because we are confused about the roles of work, play, and worship in our lives. For we tend to worship our work, to work at our play, and to play at our worship.

Forgive us. And may this special time in your presence start us on the road toward the goal of our work being a means and not an end, our play being fun, and our worship being real. Amen.

Beginning of the Fall Season

O God, in your Word we read that for everything there is a season. The summer has been a time for us to change the rhythm of our existence. Less structured schedules have permitted us to alter the pattern woven by our lives.

But now that fall fast approaches we find our pace quickening. Activities that demand our time and attention are resuming; the days seem to pass more swiftly.

As we readjust our inner and outer timetables, motivate us to give your church high priority in our lives. For we need the opportunities it provides for worship, study, support, and community. But the church also needs us to carry on its ministries by investing our time, our abilities, and our resources in its mission.

So bless us as a congregation as we begin a new program year. May we be a church and not a club, pioneers and not just settlers, an outpost as well as a sanctuary! Amen.

United Nations Day

Eternal Source of Life, who calls the worlds into being and in whose image all humankind has been created, we pause to recognize and celebrate the organization whose mission since its inception in 1945 has been to bring unity to the nations that exist on our earthly planet. For the United Nations' striving to be peacemakers and peacekeepers through dialog and arbitration rather than warfare; for its encouragement of international cooperation rather than unilateralism; for its goal of developing friendly relations among nations on the principle of equal rights and self-determination; we offer our thanks. For the United Nations' concern for the health, nutrition, education, and general welfare of the children of our world; for its response to natural or other disasters; for its efforts to care for the hungry, the homeless, and the displaced; we are grateful.

Continue, Loving God, to bless the works of this organization whose goals are in harmony with yours. And when, in any way, we as individuals or as a local church can be mini-UN's, motivate us so to be! AMEN.

Christian Education Sunday

Creator God, in whom we live and move and have our being, you who are the Holy One whose will and ways for our lives we continually seek to discern, we pause this day to recognize our need to learn more about you as well as ourselves. On this Christian Education Sunday we thank you for the tools of learning at our disposal:

- the Bible, with its progressive revelation of your nature,
- the heroes of our faith, whose lives are portrayed in both the Old and New Testaments,
- the prophets, whose teachings are preserved in our scriptures,
- the life and teachings of Jesus, whose biography and teachings were recorded by the Gospel writers,
- the writings and stories of the earliest followers of the Christ who established the Christian Church,
- the efforts of biblical scholars, whose works enable us better to understand the context in which the books of our Bible were written,
- our church, whose worship and educational offerings provide opportunities for our nurture and growth in understanding who and whose we are.

Remind us, O God, that the word disciple means "a learner," and may we rededicate ourselves to being better and more faithful disciples as we continue our pilgrimage of faith. Forbid that we ever become so smug and self-satisfied that we consider ourselves graduates rather than students who seek continued growth and knowledge about you and the Great Teacher—the one in whose spirit we pray. Amen.

Bible Presentation

God of every time and place, whom we have come to know through your still, small voice within us, through the marvels of nature, and through the ancient scriptures, we have come to worship you on this day when the importance of the Bible is recognized and affirmed. For the Bible, which is a lamp to our feet and a light to our paths, for the record of humanity's endeavors to understand your nature and how we human beings are to live, we offer our thanks. Today we recognize our gratitude to some of those whose writings and teachings have been preserved for posterity:

To Micah, who reminded us of what you require of us—to do justice, and to love kindness, and to walk humbly with you.

To Isaiah, who held out the hope for peace when he wrote, "The wolf shall live with the lamb, the leopard shall lie down with the kid, the calf and the lion and the fatling together" (Isaiah 11:6).

To the psalmist, who taught that you are "our refuge and strength, a very present help in trouble" (Psalm 46:1).

To Jesus, whose teachings remind us that when we feed the hungry, welcome the stranger, care for the sick, provide for people's basic needs—in other words, have compassion for others—we are loving and serving you.

To the many writers who remind us that you are Love.

O God, as we ponder your Word, may we, as James suggested, be not readers or hearers only, but doers, as was Jesus, the Christ, in whose spirit we pray. AMEN.

Music Appreciation

Creator God, the great Conductor of life's symphony who desires that we follow your direction, we pause to praise you for your majestic orchestration of the universe in which we live. You have given a rhythm, tempo, and beat to life that bring harmony to the ear when we follow the score before us. You cue us through difficult passages and make us feel secure in the knowledge that you can keep us and those near us together when the music is hard and the playing is rough.

We confess, however that sometimes we fail to follow your leading. We let our eyes and minds drift from the podium. We become so intent on the notes we are playing and how we want to play them that we forget about you and the other symphony members who depend upon us and who are affected by our individualized and thus, shoddy performances. The notes we play become discordant and destroy the intonation life's music is meant to have. Or, failing to watch your baton, we find ourselves out of synchronization with you and the other players.

Forgive us, we pray. And may we rededicate ourselves this day to following more closely you who are our Conductor and Jesus, the Christ, our concertmaster who has given us the note on which we are to tune the instrument we call life. AMEN.

Stewardship Sunday

Creator God, from whom springs life itself, give us this day grateful hearts for all of the blessings that have been ours in the past, that we enjoy even today, and that we know will come our way in the future.

As we count our blessings, may we not overlook this church of which we are a part. For its being here to minister to us at birth, at baptism, at confirmation, at marriage, at death; for its teaching our children and youth and us adults more about your Word and way of life; for its worship that enriches and inspires our lives; for its being a channel through which we can serve and help others both near and far away; for the community and joy of human relationships it makes possible; for the counsel and support it offers during times of personal confusion or trauma; we thank you.

But may our gratitude be deeper than mere lip service. And because a measure of the importance we attach to various facets of life is the monetary investment we are willing to make in them, stir and move us during these days of stewardship commitment to offer more than just a token or the leftovers. AMEN.

Thanksgiving Sunday

Ever-loving God of grace and God of glory, who empowers us for the living of our days, we gather in this place dedicated to your worship and service as we enter this week of Thanksgiving. We are grateful for this special season that reminds us of blessings that we sometimes take for granted. Thus, today accept our gratitude for the gifts of: thinking, hugs, acceptance, nature, kindnesses, salvation, goals, identity, vocation, ideals, nation, guidance.

Forgive us for sometimes forgetting or using unwisely these gifts that are ours. And may we be motivated to express our gratitude for your innumerable gifts by seeking to live as you would have us live—by loving you with heart, soul, mind, and strength, and our neighbor as ourselves. We pray in the spirit of another of your gifts to us, Jesus, the Christ, in whom we have seen the way, the truth, and the life. AMEN.

—

Ever-giving God, we come this morning as people who are thankful for the beauty of the earth, the splendor of the skies, and the love which from our birth over and around us lies. We come as people sustained each day by your gift of love, amazing grace, and coping power. We come as people thankful for this community seeking to be a faithful expression of the Church. We come as people grateful for this free nation in which we live. We come as people with blessings too numerous to count.

You have given us so much. Yet, sometimes when dark and difficult times enshroud us, when life's pathway is rough and rocky, when we find ourselves stumbling or falling, we forget what we have been given. We forget the assurance of your love.

We forget that you are with us in the persons of family, friends, and others who are there to help.

Open our eyes, O God, to the fullness of our lives. Keep us focused on your presence, not your perceived absence; what we have, not what we lack; on the positive, not the negative; on our needs that are met, not just our wants that are unfulfilled. Make us grateful enough not only to speak our gratitude with our lips but also to show our gratitude in the actions of our daily lives. May we celebrate this and every day by thanksliving! AMEN.

Church Anniversary

Eternal God of the past, the present, and the future, today we are especially mindful of each of these dimensions of life.

The past seems but as yesterday as we recall the history of your local church called_____: how it began as a dream in the minds of a few and was transformed into a reality that has profoundly influenced and affected the lives of us assembled here and others. For the personal commitment and the stewardship of time, energy, talents, and resources of all who have shared in its life, we give you thanks. We thank you, too, for the memories of people and events connected with the past _____ years—many joyful, some sad—but all of which are woven into the tapestry of our lives and thus have helped make us who and what we are today.

And yes, we thank you for today: for the significance of this anniversary celebration, for the opportunities to renew and strengthen relationships with you and one another, and to reaffirm our commitments to both.

Because today is the first day of the rest of our lives, make us even more receptive to your leadership and guidance in the future than we have been before. Help us as individuals and as the ones who have covenanted to be _____Church ever to remember that to be alive is to grow, and to grow is to change. Keep us faithful to the ties and traditions of the past that sustain, enrich, motivate, and challenge us. But free us from the chains of the past that make us complacent, unwilling to risk, afraid to be vulnerable. Enable us to live by the philosophy that what is past is prologue so we can face our tomorrows with openness and sensitivity—recognizing that we are responsible to share in the creation of our own and of our church's future. AMEN.

Church Centennial

God of the past, present, and future, unchanging and unchangeable throughout life's changes, we pause on this historic Sunday to sing and speak your praise. You are our help in ages past and our hope for years to come. You are our refuge and strength, a very present help in trouble. For your help and your presence within and among us, we are forever grateful.

We gather this day to thank you for the founders of and for our forebears in this church. For the gathering of this congregation and for the building of the structures in which we worship, learn, enjoy community, serve, and find ministry, each of us owes a debt of gratitude—a debt too often taken lightly or for granted, if thought about at all.

Forgive us for our insensitivity to the heritage we have been given, both spiritually and materially. Make us as concerned to grow and maintain our church in _____ as were its members in _____. As we today celebrate our past may we also rededicate ourselves to fulfilling our responsibilities of membership in our church, which are to live in all of our relationships according to the spirit and teachings of Jesus, to attend faithfully the services of worship of this church, to contribute as able to its support and to its benevolences and to share as able in its organized work.

Hear this our Centennial prayer as well as the silent prayers we now offer. Amen.

Congregational Meeting

Creative Source of all being, whose ways, will, and love were personified in the life of Jesus of Nazareth whom we call the Christ because he was willing to live as a beacon whose light would attract people to you, we, your children, have come to rededicate and renew our lives in this hour of worship.

We gather as the church, members of a community of faith committed to being the Body of Christ that tells the story and carries on the ministry of Jesus. We gather here in this sanctuary as a specific body, _____ of _____. We thank you for this community of people who have covenanted to love you with heart, soul, mind, and strength and our neighbor as ourselves and to carry on the work of the Christ in and through this local congregation.

We thank you, too, for this day on which we can discharge one of our responsibilities as members—that of reviewing, assessing, and expressing appreciation for the work accomplished in your name in the year just past and for the privilege of making decisions that will affect our future. May we as a church be even more what we are called to be: a sanctuary where we are fortified for the living of daily life, seekers who gather to learn more about you and ourselves, and a people who scatter to carry on your work and to be the church in our community and world. AMEN.

A Clergy Staff Person's First Sunday

Infinite God, whom we have come to know most fully through Jesus, we gather as the church which is called to be the Body of Christ at work in the world today, proclaiming the teachings and exemplifying the love of Jesus. For all who have been the Church in ages past and who have told the old, old story of Jesus and his love, for all who are the Church now and who strive to retell and relive that story, we offer our praise and gratitude.

This morning we thank you for your church that meets in this place to find inspiration, challenge, knowledge, wisdom, forgiveness, community, and channels for service. For its heritage of _____ years and for those today who labor to keep alive and pass on this heritage, we bless your name.

We especially feel the presence of your Spirit in our worship as we welcome _____ into our church family. May (he/she/they) feel the warmth of your acceptance and love through us as (he/she/they) begin(s) a new chapter in (his/her/their) life (lives). And may our lives be fed and enriched by _____'s ministry to and with us.

Keep us ever aware of our calling to be a church, not a club; a sanctuary, but also a springboard for service; a community in which to share both joys and concerns; a family with which to have fun but also in which to find comfort and support. Let us never forget that the church is not a building, the church is not a program, but the church is a people—and we are the church! We pray in the spirit of the one who is the cornerstone of the Church, Jesus, the Christ. AMEN.

A Clergy Staff Person's Last Sunday

Sovereign God, changeless in our ever-changing world, the Constant to whom we always can turn and upon whom we always can rely; we pause in our busyness to reestablish conscious contact with you, the Ground of our Being.

We praise and thank you for all of your gifts, many of which we are aware, many of which we take for granted. One of your gifts to us of which we are poignantly mindful is the gift of our friend and loved one, _____, who lovingly, ably, and faithfully has ministered to and with us in recent years. For her/his friendship; for her/his words of challenge and inspiration from the pulpit; for her/his acts of pastoral care; for the teaching, leadership, and example she/he has provided for our youth; we thank you.

Grant, gracious God, that as _____ begins another ministry, she/he will do so assured of your continued presence and assured that she/he carries with her/him our love and best wishes. Thank you, God, for the fact that our lives have intersected. For we are the better and richer because our paths have crossed! AMEN.

A Prayer for Peace

God of the prophet Isaiah who called nations to beat their
swords into ploughshares and their spears into pruning hooks;
God of the heavenly host who proclaimed peace and goodwill
among all; God of Jesus who said "Blessed are the peacemakers
. . ." (Matthew 5:9a) and "Be at peace with one another" (Mark
9:50b), we embrace these voices of the past as today we offer
our prayers for peace. O God, we yearn for peace in our world
filled with wars and rumors of war, in our world where
weapons of mass destruction exist, in our world where human
life often is cheap, in our world where violence sometimes is
the first response to disagreement.

We confess, Gracious One, that although we yearn for
peace, we do little to advance its cause and help make peace a
reality. May we, therefore, dedicate ourselves to
comprehending and living out the commonalities that peace
has with its enemy, war—the commonalities expressed by
former U.S. President Jimmy Carter: peace is active, not
passive; peace is doing, not waiting; peace is aggressive,
attacking; peace plans its strategy and encircles the enemy;
peace marshals its forces and storms the gates; peace gathers its
weapons and pierces the defense; peace, like war, is waged.*

Furthermore, eternal God, as we pray for peace, etch in our
lives the truth of the songwriter, "Let there be peace on earth,
but let it begin with me!" AMEN.

* Spoken at the signing of the Israeli-Egyptian Peace Treaty, April, 1979.

When Disaster Strikes

Ever-present God, to have strike close to home disasters such as the _____ that devastated neighboring communities on _____ abruptly reminds us that none of us knows what this day or tomorrow holds for him or her or friends or neighbors. The same natural laws and processes that the vast majority of time result in happiness, health, and life are the same laws and processes that sometimes result in tragedy, illness, and death.

We pause today to recognize that we are finite and that although we have relatively little control over the quantity of our lives we have great control over the quality of our lives. Therefore, may we be concerned not only about how long we live but also with how we live.

We recognize, too, that life contains the difficult, the uncertain, and the unexpected. But life also contains the strength and constancy of your love and presence that do not remove obstacles but that enable us to cope with and get through them.

Thank you for life! Thank you for your love! Amen.

When Tragedy Occurs

Loving God, constant during the changes of life, our refuge during the storms of life, our strength in times of tragedy, our hope when we feel desolated and devastated, who does not desire or will that any of your children should perish, we gather this day as a congregation in special need. You know the shock and trauma that have been ours since learning of the tragic event that affects our church family. We cannot believe that _____ is dead, but we know that we must face the reality that no longer will she/he be physically present among us.

Compassionate God, we pray for your blessing on all who grieve and suffer, all persons and families whose lives have been touched by death, especially _____. Motivate us to reach out and touch others so affected in some concrete, helpful way.

Enable us, too, to be more appreciative of the life that is ours. Since we do not know what either the present or the future holds, may we use wisely each day that dawns. May we not pave our way with so many good intentions. Rather, stir us to speak those words of love and gratitude, to give those embraces of warmth and caring, to offer our apologies and forgiveness, to do those acts of kindness, now—not later. And with the poet John Greenleaf Whittier, may we affirm:

> Within the maddening maze of things, when tossed by storm and flood,
> To one fixed trust my spirit clings; I know that God is good!
> I know not where [God's] islands lift their fronded palms in air;
> I only know I cannot drift beyond [God's] love and care.
> I know not what the future hath of marvel or surprise,
> Assured alone that life and death [God's] mercy underlies.
> AMEN.

World AIDS Day

Compassionate Creator, with sad and sobered hearts, we pause on (near) the observance of World AIDS Day to lift our voices in prayer for the victims of this worldwide pandemic. For the millions who have contracted this dread disease during their lifetime or prior to being born, for the millions who are HIV-positive and facing an uncertain future, hear our prayers for their healing.

Forgive us, merciful God, for not uniting our voices and actions with those who are seeking to slow the growth of AIDS and ease the plight of those who suffer from it. Forgive us for not encouraging our government to do more to help, for not standing up to those who equate AIDS solely with drug abuse or sexual orientation, and for refusing to support the organizations and individuals who seek to minister to those with AIDS.

Sensitize us, motivate us, and strengthen us to enter the fray of seeking to eradicate this plague that threatens our world. May we be more like Jesus, the Great Physician, who cared about and for those who were ill. In his spirit we pray. AMEN.

SIX

Pastoral Prayers for Any Sunday

Pastoral Prayers for Any Sunday

Loving God, as we turn to you in prayer, we do so in front of a mirror that reflects the images of the children in the "Peanuts" cartoons. For as we gaze at their faces we so often see ourselves.

Like Lucy: we insult other people, we laugh at others' mistakes, we destroy others' trust in us by pulling away the football when we say we will hold it in place and then pull it away just as they go to kick it—often causing them to fall. Forgive us, Forgiving One.

Like Linus: we have little confidence in ourselves, we focus our attention on what we can't do, we let others run over us, we sit in the pumpkin patch waiting for the "great pumpkin," we hold on tightly to our old, dirty, worn security blanket. Restore, our self-worth, O God, and remind us that you are the Great God who is our refuge and strength and a very present help in good as well as bad times.

Like Charlie Brown: we are wishy-washy, others tease and reject us, we think no one likes us, it's up to us to feed the dog and take care of the little sister, the ball team we manage won't listen to us. Compassionate God, may we know that we are loved by your divine love that empowers us to love ourselves and that you always are ready to listen to our prayers for guidance and help.

Like Snoopy: there is a playful nature within us and we enjoy having fun in life, we know that we are dependent upon others for many of our needs, we are a faithful, loving, and devoted friend. Holy One, in whose image we are created, may we always be like Snoopy! Amen.

—

Creative and Compassionate God, Faithful and Forgiving God, Great and Gracious One, Majestic and Merciful One; we bow before you in prayer. As we open our minds and hearts to share with you our deepest feelings and desires, we claim your promise that if we ask, we will receive, if we seek we will find, if we knock the door will be opened to us.

From the bottom of our hearts we thank you for the myriad of blessings that we enjoy, blessings too numerous to count. We are blessed with life itself, relatively good physical and mental health, resources that enable us to meet our basic needs. We are blessed with family and friends, church and nation.

Today, Creator of all, we remember those who are less fortunate than we. For those who grieve, for those who are ill, for those who are hungry and homeless, for those who are anxious and aimless, for those who are discouraged and despondent, hear our prayers. When and where it is possible, use us as answers to our prayers as we seek to be with and for those whose needs we can help. May we offer our physical presence, encouraging words, embracing hugs, shoulders on which to lean or cry, hands to help, resources to share— knowing that as we do so to others we are showing our love and gratitude to you.

As we go forth today, open our hearts, inform our minds, and guide our steps so that our lives will make a difference and bring honor and glory to you, the Source of our Being. AMEN.

—

O God, our Eternal Contemporary, who loves us as a mother and father love their child, we pause in your presence with feelings of awe, gratitude, expectation, and at times even bewilderment. Because you are infinite there is much about you that we finite beings cannot comprehend. But because you are like a parent there is much about you that we can understand.

We know that you want the best for us but that at times you cannot prevent our experiencing the worst. We know that you want us to love and serve you but that we have the freedom to rebel against you. We know that you hurt and ache when we are experiencing pain or grief.

For loving us enough to let us be persons instead of puppets, for walking with us and holding our hands when life's roads are rocky or steep, for crying with us and rejoicing with us, accept our gratitude. Thank you, God, for being our Creator, our Guide, and our Friend. AMEN.

—

Eternal One, we have come to worship and praise you for being all that you are.

You are Love. Because you love us we know that we are of value and worth. We are OK! Remind us again that our calling is to love you in return by sharing your love with others.

You are Truth. The meaning of life and the world is to be found in you. But we sometimes forget that you are our God and we are your people. And we seek life's ultimate meaning in the lesser gods that sometimes beckon.

You are Forgiveness. When we confess our sins you respond with your amazing grace that enables us to put the past behind us and to begin again.

You are Strength. Your power is latent within us just waiting to be tapped. To do so is to find that we are able to do more than we realize or than we thought we could. For this we are grateful.

You are Consolation. Hurt, pain, and despair seem indigenous to our lives. But you directly, and indirectly through our loved ones and friends, bring us comfort and lead us through the shadows of life until we are back in the sunlight again. Thank you!

We pray in the spirit of your incarnation, Jesus, the Christ. AMEN.

—

Well, God, another week has passed and a new one begins. So at this juncture we want to interrupt our personal, family, and business routines long enough to spend a special hour with you and your friends. In fact, Creator God, we do not view this hour as an interruption. Rather, we feel it is vital to our lives. For here we are challenged to think about a Supreme Being, not just lesser gods; absolutes, not just relativities; ideals, not just ideas; persons, not just things; quality of existence, not just quantity; what is right, not just what is expedient.

So while we are here enable us to listen, to evaluate, and to be motivated to leave this sanctuary and live this new week in such a way that the Christ will be reflected in our words and actions. AMEN.

—

God of this and every day, the smell of the grass after the rain, the iris blooming in our gardens, the singing of the birds, the smiles on the faces of our families and friends remind us of how great you are and how good life is! So on this your day we have come into this setting to acknowledge and praise you for your presence in our world and in our lives. For it is your presence that enables even storm clouds to have silver linings and that enables us to find joy even in the midst of despair.

We thank you, Fountain of life, for our faith—a faith that makes a difference in our lives. For ours is a faith that provides an example and pattern for daily living. Our faith challenges us to ponder the life and teachings of Jesus and therein to find suggestions for our lives—such as to love rather than hate, to serve rather than use, to be involved rather than apathetic, to give as well as receive.

Today we profess this faith through the words we speak and sing and by our presence here. Forbid that our profession will cease at the conclusion of this hour. Rather, may the remainder of today and this new week find our professions translated into our actions as we go about the living of each day. AMEN.

—

Great, gracious, and giving God, we glorify you because of who you are and whose we are. You are our Creator, the ultimate Source of life and love and the other blessings we sometimes take for granted, such as the abilities to see a waterfall, hear an infant, taste warm bread, touch an animal, and smell a rose. We have been created with a God-shaped vacuum within us, and we drift aimlessly and hopelessly on the sea of life until we invite your spirit to fill the vacuum, thereby giving us the buoyancy and stability needed for us to move toward the goals we have set.

For offering to bring our lives order from chaos, wholeness from fragmentation, hope from despair, forgiveness from guilt, self-worth from self-loathing, generosity from selfishness, caring from apathy; thank you, Redeeming One.

Walk with us as we enter this new week. By your grace enable us to see possibilities rather than problems, windows of opportunity rather than closed doors, persons rather than things, life rather than mere existence. AMEN.

—

Ever-calling, ever-beckoning God, who accepts us as we are but who also knows the persons we can become, we pause in our worship to share with you our feelings of gratitude, contrition, and resolve. We are grateful for your acceptance and love that enable us better to accept and love ourselves. For only when we do so can we accept and love others. We thank you as well for the other innumerable blessings we enjoy: family, friends, health, food, shelter, talents, church, nation, coping power.

When we reflect on who we are because of the gifts we enjoy we become more mindful of whose we are. Yet, we confess that too often we fail to live as though we are yours. Thus, for our willful sins and failures both of commission and omission as well as for our unthinking and unintentional wrongdoings, we ask your forgiveness.

May our having been in this place this morning and having shared in words and music that speak of you give us the resolve to enter this new week more sensitive to the fact that you have called us to be your children, your servants, and your witnesses. Although we are free to shut our ears to and turn our backs on your calling, may we, in love that is a response to your love for us, say, "Here am I, dear God, use me!" AMEN.

—

O God, whose eye is always on the sparrow and on us because we are special and precious in your sight, we confess that our view of you and the world in which we live sometimes is warped and filtered by what we see through the eyes of television. For so often these and other media deceive us into thinking that human life is cheap, that the end always justifies the means, that violent actions bring prompt results, and that more and bigger always are better.

Thus, we thank you for this hour and this place that help us put life back into proper perspective. For here we are confronted by your Word and reminded that our lives should be focused on what is true, honorable, just, pure, lovely, and gracious. Here we are reminded of and can feel again the strength with which you fill our lives—strength that enables us to cope with whatever comes our way.

Thank you for our church, loving God, because it calls us to worship you, refocus our lives, and then to leave your sanctuary and go out to live the fully human and humane life you have created us to live—a life patterned after the one who knew you more completely and saw you more clearly than has any other person—Jesus, the Christ, our Savior. AMEN.

—

Eternal God, who is One and Universal, Creator of all—red and yellow, black, brown, and white—we pause to worship and praise you. Loving God, you are known by different names and worshiped in different ways. Yet, you are the God of East and West, North and South.

We gather today to confess that we and others have not been the best of your children. We have let race and nationality and culture and sex and age and forms of government and the resources of our planet divide and create barriers among us. We have forsaken the ancient teachings of the prophets Isaiah and Micah and continued to rely on violence or warfare to settle our differences. Your forgiveness, therefore, is needed by all of us, wherever we live in your world.

Gracious God, whom we have come to know and love through the one who was called the Prince of Peace, may negotiations occur so that lives will not be lost on the battlefields, in the air, and in cities, towns, or villages anywhere in the world due to war. For we know that you desire that we love and have concern and compassion even for those who may be our enemies.

As we pray for the needs of our world, we also pray for the needs of our individual lives. Forgive our sins; calm our anxieties; strengthen our resolve; keep us faithful, hopeful, and helpful as we go about the living of this new week. We pray in the spirit of the one who said, "I am with you always, to the end of the age" (Matthew 28:20b). AMEN.

—

Eternal, ever-present God, Creator of the world and giver of life to all who dwell therein, Parent of all nations and races, as the sun's warm rays call forth a blossom from a bud, so your still, small voice calls forth the best that is in us. Thus, this morning we pause in your presence—attracted by the warmth of your love and desire to have our lives remolded so they will better fit into your will and ways.

Forgive us, gracious God, for forgetting that you can help us transform and remake our lives. Our hatred can be turned into love, our ingratitude into thanksgiving, our insensitivity into feeling and caring, our anxiety into confidence, our pessimism into optimism, our stress into release from tension, our intentions into deeds, our apathy into action, our parochialism into universal concern, our myopia into farsightedness, our prejudice into tolerance, our penchant for doing evil into a penchant for doing good.

Make us aware, therefore, of the areas of our lives in which changes are needed. And with your leading and inspiration, enable us to address ourselves to this task. AMEN.

Eternal Spirit of the universe, who began the process of creation and thus is the source of our very lives, you who are to us like a loving father and a compassionate mother; we your children pause in reverence to praise and thank you for the gift of life.

For talents to use, for the freedom to choose; for the capacity to cope, for the blessing of hope; for loved ones for whom we can care, for others with whom we can share; we express our gratitude.

We confess, O God, that at times—in fact, too often—we do not use our lives wisely. We let our talents rust or go to waste. We fracture relationships. We hurt others by what we do or say, or fail to say or do. We go against what our conscience tells us is right. We are myopic, thinking only of ourselves or our immediate world. We selfishly accumulate but do not give out of gratitude to those whose need is apparent.

Forgive us, forgiving God. And on this, the first day of the rest of our lives, help us to begin to right the wrongs and repair the damages that have created barriers between ourselves and you and ourselves and others. Thus, gracious God, our prayer at the beginning of this new day and week is that we will be better children of yours and better brothers and sisters of one another. Amen.

SEVEN

Prayers before
Church Gatherings

Prayers before Church Gatherings

Ever-beckoning God, who has called us into the church to accept the cost and joy of discipleship, we thank you for this local expression of the universal Church. May we feel your presence within and among us as we meet on this occasion and deal with the agenda before us. May our deliberations and all of our decisions be acceptable to you, whom we seek to serve. Amen.

—

As we gather, gracious God, we pause to reflect on the importance of this church in our lives. For the opportunities of worship, education, service, and community it provides; for the support it offers in times of crisis and need; for the ties that bind our hearts in Christian love; we praise and thank you. May our lives be strengthened and enriched because we have been together in this time and place. We pray in the spirit of the one who is the Great Head of the Church, Jesus, the Christ. Amen.

—

God of grace and God of glory, pour your power upon us who have accepted responsibilities in this church and who have gathered to discharge them. Grant us wisdom, grant us courage for the business of this hour and for the living of all of our days. May we ever hold before us the goals of your realm so that we will not fail others or you by what we do or fail to do. For we desire to serve you, whom we adore. Amen.

—

Ever-living God, who has given us the church for our instruction and inspiration, be with us as we seek to be faithful members of the Body of Christ. Thank you, ever-giving God, for the gifts you have given us. May we use them in your service and to the end that your realm will come and your will be done on earth as it is in heaven. AMEN.

—

God of Abraham and Sarah, God of Moses and Miriam, God of the prophets, and God of Jesus; we acknowledge that you are our God, too, and that we are your people. Individually, and corporately as this church, may we seek to fulfill what you require of us: to do justice, and to love kindness, and to walk humbly with you. AMEN.

—

O God, who has called the worlds into being and created us in your image as persons who can love, feel, reason, and will: may we use each of these attributes as we share in the ministry of our church. May our labors build up this body which seeks to tell the story and carry on the ministry of Jesus, who was called "The One for Others" and in whose spirit and for whose sake we pray. AMEN.

—

God of all goodness, faithful and changeless amid all of life's changes, our help and comfort when all else fails, and who promises to be present when even two or three have gathered in your name; bestow upon us your Spirit so that the words of our mouths, the meditations of our hearts, and the actions of our lives will be acceptable to you, our Rock and our Redeemer. AMEN.

EIGHT

Prayers before Community Gatherings

Prayers before Community Gatherings

O Holy One, whom we call by different names because we are a diverse people, but who has called us to live together in community, respecting the uniqueness and gifts of each and every person; grant your presence among us as we share in this significant occasion. Give us ears that hear one another, voices that speak the truth in love, minds that make sense out of confusion or disorder, and hearts that seek to fulfill your purposes. AMEN.

—

Creator and creating God, you who have the whole world in your hands, we claim to be one nation, under you, and that you are the One in whom we trust. May the words we speak and the actions we take while we are together reflect what we profess. AMEN.

—

Eternal Spirit of the universe, we gather as an organization committed to making our community, nation, and world better places in which to live. Bless us, we pray, as we meet this day. May our presence and participation inform, enrich, and inspire our lives and also challenge us anew to live out the principles and vision that we share in common. AMEN.

—

God of our forebears, God of our mothers and fathers, and our God; we are mindful this day of the heritage left by those who founded and those who were a part of this community in years gone by. May we not take for granted what we have been given, and may we be responsible citizens who strive continually to make liberty and justice a reality for all. Amen.

—

Fountain of life, light, and truth, you have so created us that we realize in the depths of our beings that none of us is an island and that none of us wants to walk alone. We have experienced that our hearts are restless until they rest in you and in one another. Therefore, we thank you for all who have assembled in this place and pray that our being together will enhance each of our lives. Amen.

—

Source of all existence and Sustainer of all the worlds that are, make us aware that even though you are a High and Holy God you also are a God who is present within and among us. We are aware that you have called us to love you and one another, and we pray that you will remind us anew that love, to be love, must be expressed in action. Thus, may our being together inspire us to put our love into practice through lives of service to all whose lives touch ours. Amen.

—

All-encompassing God, whose we are and whose ways are to be reflected in every realm of life; grant that we will not think of you and be concerned to do your bidding only when we are in our houses of worship. Even as we meet as a civic body may we acknowledge that we are not the masters of our fates and the captains of our souls, that we are not owners but stewards of the gifts of life, and that we are the freest when we align our wills with yours. May this be reflected in what we do and say in the moments to come. AMEN.

NINE

Personal Prayers for
the Worship Leader

Prayers of Gratitude

Ever-giving and generous God, who loves me not because of my merits but just because I am; I pause in your presence, overwhelmed by the blessings that are mine. Life itself, family, friends, food, home, church, community, the marvels and beauty of creation, and other blessings too numerous to mention fill my life to overflowing. Keep me, I pray, from ever taking for granted what I enjoy. And may I always remember that I am the caregiver and caretaker, not the owner, of all that seems to be mine. In gratitude and humility I pray. AMEN.

—

Caring Creator, whose love surrounds me, whose strength supports me, whose truth enlightens me, and whose spirit leads me; you have given me an example and pattern for my daily living in Jesus, the Christ. For his life and teachings, for his showing me the way, and for his revelation that you are always with me, I offer my heart felt thanks. May my actions and my attitudes reflect my gratitude! AMEN.

—

O Eternal Contemporary, whom I have come to know and love through the marvels and beauty of your creation; through your child Jesus, the Christ; and through your ever-present and empowering Holy Spirit: thank you for being a God who is not only beyond me but also within me; a God who cannot spare me from life but who can and will help me through life; and a God who loves me just as I am. May my gratitude be expressed as I seek to make my actions consistent with the faith I feel in my heart and profess with my lips. AMEN.

Loving God, my Comforter when I am comfortless, my Friend when I am friendless, my Healer when I am hurting, my Helper when I feel helpless, my Hope when I am hopeless, my Salvation when I sin; you are caring when I am careless, compassionate when I am compassionless, faithful when I am faithless, merciful when I am merciless: how great you are! Thank you for loving me even when I am unlovable and for walking with me each step of life's way. With my heart filled with gratitude I sing with the psalmist: "Bless God, O my soul, and all that is within me, bless God's holy name. Bless God, O my soul, and do not forget all God's benefits" (Psalm 103:1–2). AMEN.

—

Persuasive Presence, who loves and cares for me as a shepherd loves and cares for the flock, awaken me anew to your presence within and around me. You seek me when I go astray; you pick me up when I fall; you carry me when I am weak; you love me when I am unlovable. For your unmerited love and amazing grace I praise your name and express my heartfelt gratitude. AMEN.

—

Eternal God, whose mercy encompasses the universe and whose love embraces all humankind, as a part of your creation in this time and place I pause to praise you for the world in which I live and for all of the blessings that I enjoy. To reflect my gratitude, I rededicate myself to loving people and using things rather than loving things and using people. For every human being is your child and thus my sister or brother. AMEN.

Prayers for Forgiveness

Faithful and forgiving God, who loves me as I am as well as for whom I can become, who sees through my problems and envisions my potential; thank you for enabling me both to be and to become. For my past and present sins of commission and omission, I ask your pardon. Enabled by your amazing grace, may I become the person you want me to be. AMEN.

—

Righteous God, I confess that in your presence and among your other children I have sinned in thought, word, and deed. Like Paul of old, " For I do not do the good I want, but the evil I do not want is what I do" (Romans 7:19). But you, compassionate God, are like a merciful mother or a forgiving father who is more willing to accept and love me than I am willing to accept and love myself. You desire to build me up even as I continue to tear myself down. In these moments may your love so penetrate my hard heart that I will not self-destruct but begin to be rebuilt by the power of your ever-present and empowering Holy Spirit. AMEN.

—

Patient, persistent, and pursuing God, whose still, small voice calls me again and again to move from death to life—that is, from faithlessness to faithfulness, from selfishness to generosity, from grudge bearing to forgiving, from living in the past to embracing the present—forgive my stubbornness and for being so slow to respond to you.

May the gentle breath of your spirit so refresh and renew every part of my being that my hands better will serve you, my lips more often praise you, and my heart more consistently love you. Thus, may I become more like Jesus, in whose spirit I pray. AMEN.

—

Loving God, who continually invites me to accept your guiding grace, forgive me for the times when I have turned my back on you. May I be inspired to say "yes" to your will and ways so that I will become more the person you want me to be—one who seeks to emulate Jesus, the Christ, in whose spirit I pray. AMEN.

Prayers for Guidance and Help

Concerned and caring God, how much I need the assurance of your presence and help. I am tired and discouraged. I feel weighted down by the burdens of my life. So inscribe within my heart the words of your prophet: "Have you not known? Have you not heard? God is the everlasting God, the Creator of the ends of the earth. God does not faint or grow weary; God's understanding is unsearchable. God gives power to the faint, and strengthens the powerless. Even youths will faint and be weary, and the young will fall exhausted; but those who wait for God shall renew their strength, they shall mount up with wings like eagles, they shall run and not be weary, they shall walk and not faint" (Isaiah 40:28–31). Mindful of this promise, I now can deal with this day! AMEN.

—

Great God of Hope, I pause before you because I know that you will hear my prayer. At this difficult time in my life I need assurance because I am anxious, direction because I am drifting, energy because I feel empty, love because I feel lonely. Open my heart, Holy One, to the empowering and refreshing breath of your Spirit. Open my eyes, Enlightening One, to the paths I should take. For you, O God, are my refuge and strength, and a very present help in trouble. This I have learned especially through Jesus, the Christ, my Savior, in whose spirit I pray. AMEN.

—

Great and Gracious God, who taught me through your child Jesus that I am to love you with my mind as well as my heart, soul, and strength; thank you for the privilege of asking, questioning, and even doubting what I have been taught. As I struggle with my faith, may I move ever closer to the truth which sets me free—the truth I experience in the one who is the Way, the Truth, and the Life, even Jesus, the Christ. AMEN.

Other Books from The Pilgrim Press

Praying by Heart
Prayers for Personal Devotion and Public Worship
KAY BESSLER NORTHCUTT

"These are not sentimental or jargon-ridden 'care and share' outpourings. They aim to be directly about their business of carrying on the conversation between a self-disclosing God and the people collected. The agent will be the pastor who prays off the pages, using words by an expressive author who has the grace to move herself offstage and let the prayers be those of 'us' and not 'me.' Let us pray."—Martin E. Marty from the Foreword

ISBN 0-8298-1285-7/paper/128 pg/**$13.00**

Hear Our Prayer
Resources for Worship and Devotions
GLEN E. RAINSLEY

This practical and useful resource is a poetic and moving collection of calls to worship, opening prayers, prayers of confession, words of assurance, prayers of dedication, benedictions, pastoral prayers, and introductions to silent prayer.

ISBN 0-8298-1145-1/paper/208 pp./**$15.00**

Trumpet in Zion

Worship Resources, Year A

Linda H. Hollies

Trumpet in Zion, Year A addresses God in the voice, verbiage, and expression of African Americans in worship. Based on the Revised Common Lectionary, this resource offers clergy, worship planners, and lay leaders the opportunity to utilize the Bible in new and engaging ways with their congregations.

isbn 0-8298-1410-8/paper/214 pages/**$14.00**

Trumpet in Zion

Worship Resources, Year B

Linda H. Hollies

Following the structure of the Revised Common Lectionary, this resource includes calls to worship, prayers of confession, words of assurance, responsive readings, offertory invitations, and blessings for each Sunday. It is also highly adaptable, making it an ideal resource for congregations who do not follow the lectionary.

isbn 0-8298-1477-9/paper/214/**$14.00**

Taught by Love

Worship Resources for Year A
LAVON BAYLER

This trilogy provides calls to worship, invocations, hymns, and more. All designed on the Revised Common Lectionary, these resources can be used by those who do not use the lectionary to enhance worship.

ISBN 0-8298-1235-0/paper/344 pages/**$16.95**

Led by Love

Worship Resources for Year B
LAVON BAYLER

ISBN 0-8298-1124-9/paper/344 pages/**$17.00**

Gathered by Love

Worship Resources for Year C
LAVON BAYLER

ISBN 0-8298-1008-0/paper/344 pages/**$16.95**

To order these or any other books from The Pilgrim Press, call or write to:

The Pilgrim Press
700 Prospect Avenue East
Cleveland, Ohio 44115-1100

Phone orders: 800.537.3394 • Fax orders: 216.736.2206

Please include shipping charges of $4.00 for the first book and $.75 for each additional book.

Or order from our Web sites at <www.pilgrimpress.com> and <www.ucpress.com>.

Prices subject to change without notice.